# PRAYERS

FOR

# HEALING

# PRAYERS
### —— FOR ——
# HEALING

## 365 Blessings, Poems,
## & Meditations
### *from* Around the World

Edited by MAGGIE OMAN

Introduction by
THE DALAI LAMA

Foreword by
LARRY DOSSEY

🕉

**Conari Press**

First Published in 1999 by Conari Press
an imprint of Red/Wheel Weiser, LLC
with offices at:
500 Third Street, Suite 230
San Francisco, CA 94107
www.redwheelweiser.com

*Cover Photograph:* Courtesy of Photonica.
Serpent Gourd by Masaaki Kazama
*Cover and Interior Design:* Suzanne Albertson
*Interior Illustrations:* Roger Montoya

ISBN: 978-1-57324-522-7

**Library of Congress Cataloging-in-Publication Data**
Prayers for healing : 365 blessings, poems, and meditations
from around the world / edited by Maggie Oman : foreword by
Larry Dossey : introduction by The Dalai Lama.
p.     cm.
Includes index.
ISBN 1-57324-522-4 (pb)
ISBN 1-57324-089-3 (hc)
1. Spiritual healing—Prayer-books and devotions—English.
I. Oman, Maggie, 1958-
BL65.M4P65     1997
291.4'33—dc21                    97-19158
CIP

*Printed in the United States of America*
RRD   10  9  8  7

*This book is dedicated with love*
to my mother,
Mary Jane Burruss Oman,
and the memory of my father,
Frederick Paul Oman

# PRAYERS *for* HEALING

THE ETERNAL QUEST OF HUMANKIND HAS BEEN to reach out to something greater and wiser than our limited self—whether conceived as God, Goddess, Allah, Brahman, the Absolute. Today this impulse is deeply felt, and is perhaps more urgent than ever before.

As we enter a new millennium, most people realize that we are going to require more than intellectual knowledge and technical expertise to meet the great challenges that lie ahead. That is where prayer comes in.

Prayer helps us contact sources of inspiration and wisdom that transcend the rational, analytical side of the mind. Prayer provides a sense of hope and meaning—the certainty that we are part of a pattern that is purposeful and intelligent. Without this awareness, life is not just unsatisfying, it can be unendurable. That is one reason the former minister of culture of France, the late Andre Malraux, said that the twenty-first century will be spiritual or it will not be at all.

*Prayers for Healing* can help us deepen the spiritual dimension in our lives. It can help us connect with the Absolute, with the Earth that sustains us, and with each other.

What could be more important?

—*Larry Dossey, M.D.,* author of
*Prayer is Good Medicine* and
*Healing Words: The Power of Prayer
and The Practice of Medicine*

WHEN PEOPLE ARE OVERWHELMED BY ILLNESS, we must give them physical relief, but it is equally important to encourage the spirit through a constant show of love and compassion. It is shameful how often we fail to see that what people desperately require is human affection. Deprived of human warmth and a sense of value, other forms of treatment prove less effective. Real care of the sick does not begin with costly procedures, but with the simple gift of affection and love.

In the practice of healing, a kind heart is as valuable as medical training, because it is the source of happiness for both oneself and others. Not only do other people respond to kindness even when medicine is ineffective, but cultivating a kind heart is a cause of our own good health. Similarly, inner peace can be found in prayer and meditation, but it is also profoundly important that we bring that inner peace to bear in practical ways in the generous service of others.

There is a connection here with the practice of non-violence. Nonviolence is something more positive, more meaningful than the mere absence of violence. It means to respect the rights of others, to be concerned about their well-being, based on a sense of compassion. Today, there is a growing global awareness of what this implies, for the application of nonviolence is not restricted merely to other human beings. It also has to do with ecology, the environment and our relations with all the other living beings with whom we share the planet. Since human beings are basically gentle by nature, I feel that we should not only maintain gentle, peaceful relations with our fellow human beings, but that it is also very important to extend the same kind of attitude towards our environment and the creatures who naturally live in harmony with it.

This book contains a collection of prayers for healing from different traditions. I believe it is essential that we extend our understanding of each other's spiritual practices and prayers. This is not necessarily in order that we can adopt them ourselves, but because to do so increases our opportunities for mutual respect.

Sometimes, too, we encounter something in another tradition that helps us better appreciate something in our own. Consequently, I hope that people of all faiths as well as those who do not believe in a religion will find inspiration and understanding here that in some way contributes to their own inner peace. And I pray that through that inner peace they too will become better human beings and help create a happier, more peaceful world.

> May all who are sick and ill
> Quickly be freed from their illness,
> And may every disease in the world
> Never occur again.
>
> And as long as space endures,
> As long as there are beings to be found,
> May I continue likewise to remain
> To soothe the sufferings of those who live.

—*The Dalai Lama*

# LETTER OF THE HEART

THE TIME SPENT WORKING ON *Prayers for Healing* has been a deeply healing and transformative period for me personally, and whether the book that you now hold is a cause of that, or the result of that, I do not know. What I do know is that it is impossible to read the words, in some cases centuries old, of fellow human beings entreating, praising, and questioning the Divine entity of their understanding without being moved—and even profoundly changed.

I believe one reason for that, perhaps *the* reason for that, is because we are our most authentic, essential selves when communicating with a deity whose existence we can know, but not prove; for when we pray, truly and even desperately reach out to our God, we are stripped to our souls. When sincerely attempting to make a connection with Spirit, we in effect transcend our own humanity and become spirit—some would say, remind ourselves of our true identity as spirit—acknowledging as we are when we pray that there is another, unseen realm of significance, and that it is the arena of ultimate meaning.

That said, there is a raw beauty in the myriad, and very human, modes of expressing prayers—and it has been my desire to include a full range of voices, from the elegance of Sir Thomas More's plea for the forgiveness of his enemies to the directness of Marian Wright Edelman's dissection of pretense, from the simplicity of Basho's reflection on changing perceptions to the rousing rhythm of Martin Luther King's call for a collective vision of equality. Their voices are the reflections of our own struggles and dreams; their prayers are our prayers.

To better place these letters of the heart into the human context in which they were written—and to help us connect to the actual men and women who wrote or inspired them—I have included relevant historical dates of reference for some of the prayers included here. They are also organized according to season, in the hope that being mindful of nature's cycles will foster healing in our wounded collective relationship with the earth. This volume can be used as a daily meditation tool beginning at whatever date you happen to encounter it, or flipped through at random until a particular piece speaks to you. As Madeleine L'Engle reminds us, the root word for "heal," *hale,* is the same for the word "whole"—and thus the subjects explored herein speak to the whole of our existence, encompassing ourselves as individuals and as a society, our environment and the creatures with which we share it.

It is my heartfelt prayer that readers of *Prayers for Healing* will encounter at least one prayer, on at least one day, that will resonate deeply within them and contribute to their own healing, in whatever facet or circumstance of life that it may be needed. My wish for all of us is best expressed in the words of Thich Nhat Hanh: "May all beings learn how to nourish themselves with joy each day."

—*Maggie Oman*
*San Francisco, California*

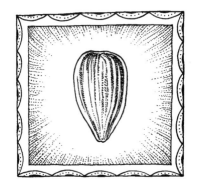

WINTER

**December 21**

*Winter Solstice*

> In the beginning was`the Tao.
> All things issue from it;
> all things return to it.
>
> To find the origin,
> trace back the manifestations.
> When you recognize the children
> and find the mother,
> you will be free of sorrow.
>
> If you close your mind in judgments
> and traffic with desires,
> your heart will be troubled.
> If you keep your mind from judging
> and aren't led by the senses,
> your heart will find peace.
>
> Seeing into darkness is clarity.
> Knowing how to yield is strength.
> Use your own light
> and return to the source of light.
> This is called practicing eternity.
>
> —*Lao-Tzu*
> *Translated by Stephen Mitchell*

## December 22

*English novelist George Eliot*
*(Mary Ann Evans)*
*dies in 1880*

> May I reach
> That purest heaven, be to other souls
> The cup of strength in some great agony,
> Enkindle generous ardour, feed pure love,
> Be the sweet presence of a good diffused,
> And in diffusion ever more intense!
> So shall I join the choir invisible
> Whose music is the gladness of the world.

> —*George Eliot*

## December 23

> The tree in winter is like
> The lines upon my father's face
> Or like the paths I tried to take
> When I was young searching
> For one clear way to understanding.
> In every branch I found
> A smaller branch leading me
> Toward many ends and many sorrows.
> Too fragile to bear my weight,
> All my branches broke

And I fell to the earth confused.
I saw the tree in winter
Reaching toward the sky
With bare branches tangled
Like so many paths and yet
Each path had a purpose,
Leading back to the roots of the tree.

—*Nancy Wood*

**December 24**
*Hanukkah*
*(date varies)*

How wonderful, O Lord, are the works of your
        hands!
The heavens declare Your glory,
the arch of sky displays Your handiwork.
In Your love You have given us the power
to behold the beauty of Your world
robed in all its splendor.
The sun and the starts, the valleys and hills,
the rivers and lakes all disclose Your presence.
The roaring breakers of the sea tell of Your awesome
        might;
the beasts of the field and the birds of the air

bespeak Your wondrous will.
In Your goodness You have made us able to hear
the music of the world. The voices of loved ones
reveal to us that You are in our midst.
A divine voice sings through all creation.

—Jewish prayer

## December 25
*Christmas Day*

Lord Jesus Christ, you are the gentle moon and joyful
stars, that watch over the darkest night. You are the
source of all peace, reconciling the whole universe to
the Father. You are the source of all rest, calming troubled hearts, and bringing sleep to weary bodies. You are
the sweetness that fills our minds with quiet joy, and
can turn the worst nightmares into dreams of heaven.
May I dream of your sweetness, rest in your arms, be at
one with your Father, and be comforted in the knowledge that you always watch over me.

—Erasmus

## December 26

This being human is a guest house.
Every morning is a new arrival.

A joy, a depression, a meanness,
some momentary awareness comes
as an unexpected visitor.

Welcome and entertain them all!
Even if they're a crowd of sorrows,
who violently sweep your house
empty of its furniture,
still, treat each guest honorably.
He may be clearing you out
for some new delight.

The dark thought, the shame, the malice,
meet them at the door laughing,
and invite them in.

Be grateful for whoever comes,
because each has been sent
as a guide from beyond.

> —*Rumi*
> *Translated by Coleman Barks*

## December 27

Now that the sun has set,
I sit and rest, and think of you.
Give my weary body peace.
Let my legs and arms stop aching.
Let my nose stop sneezing,
Let my head stop thinking.
Let me sleep in your arms.

—*Dinka, date unknown*

## December 28

From that which we fear, make us fearless.
O bounteous One, assist us with your aid.

May the atmosphere we breathe
breathe fearlessness into us:
fearlessness on earth
and fearlessness in heaven!
May fearlessness surround us
above and below!

May we be without fear
by night and by day!
Let all the world be my friend!

—*Atharva Veda XIX*

### December 29

Infinite Spirit, when I pray each day
for shelter for the homeless,
let me not ignore the pet without a home;

As I ask for protection for those in areas
of turmoil and unrest,
let me not forget endangered species of life;

When I pray that the hungry be fed,
let me be mindful
that all God's creatures have need of sustenance;

As I ask Divine assistance for those afflicted
by fire, flood, earthquake, storm or drought,
let me remember that this includes every living thing;

In seeking miracle cures for human disease,
may I also speak for the well-being of the planet itself.

Let the words of my mouth,
the meditations of my heart
and the actions of my life be as one,
that I may live each day in harmony
with Mother Earth. Amen.

*—Jennie Frost Butler*

## December 30

After a while you learn the subtle difference
Between holding a hand
And chaining a soul.
And you learn that love doesn't mean leaning
And company doesn't mean security.
And you begin to learn
That kisses aren't compromises
And presents aren't promises.
And you begin to accept your defeats
With your head up and your eyes ahead
With the grace of a woman or a man
Not the grief of a child.
And you learn to build all your loads on today
Because tomorrow's ground is too uncertain for plans
And futures have a way of falling down in midflight.
After a while you learn that even sunshine burns if
you ask too much.
So you plant your own garden
And decorate your own soul
Instead of waiting for someone to buy you flowers.
And you learn that you really can endure
That you really are strong.
And you really do have worth.
And you learn. And you learn.
With every failure you learn.

—*Anonymous*

### December 31

The last day of what has been an uneasy and painful
year for me. I look forward to dawn tomorrow and, as
the days get longer, to begin to feel my way into
renascence. It is not strange though it is mysterious that
our "New Year" comes at the darkest time in the sea-
sonal cycle. When there is personal darkness, when
there is pain to be overcome, when we are forced to
renew ourselves against all the odds, the psychic energy
required simply to survive has tremendous force, as
great as that of a bulb pushing up through icy ground
in spring, so after the overcoming, there is extra energy,
a flood of energy that can go into creation.

—*May Sarton*

### January 1
*New Year's Day*

We look with uncertainty
Beyond the old choices for
Clear-cut answers
To a softer, more permeable aliveness
Which is every moment
At the brink of death;
For something new is being born in us
If we but let it.

We stand at a new doorway,
Awaiting that which comes...
Daring to be human creatures.
Vulnerable to the beauty of existence.
Learning to love.

—*Anne Hillman*

## January 2

There is nothing I can give you
which you do have not;
But there is much, very much, that
while I cannot give it, you can take.

No heaven can come to us unless our hearts
find rest in today. Take heaven!
No peace lies in the future which is not hidden
in this present instant. Take peace!

The gloom of the world is but a shadow.
Behind it, yet within reach, is joy.
There is a radiance and glory in the darkness, could
we but see,
and to see, we have only to look. I beseech you
to look.

—*Fra Giovanni*

**January 3**

> Help me to let go of my preoccupations
> with the future.
> Give me the strength to stop
> my futile attempts
> to predict and control the future.
> Let me see no value in my plan
> of what the future should be.
> Rid me of my senseless questions
> about tomorrow
> And of all my desires to manipulate
> and control others.
>
> Remind me that my fears and uncertainties
> of tomorrow are only related to
> my unfounded fear of You.
>
> Help me be still
> help me listen and love.
>
> Awaken me to the truth of Your Presence
> being only in the now of this moment.
> Lift me up into Your Arms
> and remind me that I am Your Creation,
> and that I am the Perfection of Love.
> Help me to acknowledge that I am Your Messenger
> of Love, and free me to shine
> Your Light everywhere.

Let me feel Your Freedom within me, and
     let me laugh at the illusions
     that my ego once made
     me feel were so real.

Let me be the Light; let me be joy; let me know
     that I am
     the reflection of You wherever I am,
     and wherever I go.

                    —*Gerald G. Jampolsky*

## January 4

The world is new each morning—that is God's gift,
and a man should believe he is reborn each day.

                    —*Israel Ben Eliezer*


## January 5

TODAY—Mend a quarrel. Search out a forgotten
friend. Dismiss suspicion and replace it with trust.
Write a love letter. Share some treasure. Give a soft
answer. Encourage youth. Manifest your loyalty in a
word or a deed.

TODAY—Keep a promise. Find the time. Forego a grudge. Forgive an enemy. Listen. Apologize if you were wrong. Try to understand. Flout envy. Examine your demands on others. Think first of someone else. Appreciate, be kind, be gentle. Laugh a little more.

TODAY—Deserve confidence. Take up arms against malice. Decry complacency. Express your gratitude. Worship your God. Gladden the heart of a child. Take pleasure in the beauty and wonder of the earth. Speak it again. Speak it still again. Speak it still once again.

—*Anonymous*

### January 6

Everyone has a spirit that can be refined, a body that can be trained in some manner, a suitable path to follow. You are here for no other purpose than to realize your inner divinity and manifest your innate enlightenment. Foster peace in your own life and apply the Art of Peace to all that you encounter.

—*Morihei Ueshiba*

## January 7

I have no other helper than you, no other father, I
    pray to you.
Only you can help me. My present misery is too
    great.
Despair grips me, and I am at my wit's end.
O Lord, Creator, Ruler of the World, Father.
I thank you that you have brought me through.

How strong the pain was—but you were stronger.
How deep the fall was—but you were even deeper.
How dark the night was—but you were the noonday
    sun in it.
You are our father, our mother, our brother, and our
    friend.

*—African prayer*

## January 8

The thought manifests as the word;
The word manifests as the deed;
The deed develops into habit;
And habit hardens into character.
    So watch the thought and its ways with care,
And let it spring from love
Born out of concern for all beings.

*—The Buddha*

## January 9

Let sleep not come upon thy languid eyes
Before each daily action thou hast scanned;
What's done amiss, what done, what left undone;
From first to last examine all, and then
Blame what is wrong, in what is right rejoice.

—*Attributed to Pythagoras*

## January 10

The threat to our salvation is the clash of peoples:
Jews and Arabs,
offspring of a single father,
separated in youth by jealousy,
in adolescence by fear,
in adulthood by power,
in old age by habit.
It is time to break these habits of hate
and create new habits:
habits of the heart
that will awake within us
the causeless love of redemption and peace.

—*Rabbi Rami M. Shapiro*

## January 11

Come, my Light, and illumine my darkness.
Come, my Life, and revive me from death.
Come, my Physician, and heal my wounds.
Come, Flame of divine love, and burn up the thorns
of my sins, kindling my heart with the flame of
your love.
Come, my King, sit upon the throne of my heart and
reign there.
For you alone are my King and my Lord.

*—Saint Dimitrii of Rostov*

## January 12

*(Self-baptism for the morning; to be recited while sprinkling water on the head.)*

O Waters, give us health, bestow on us
Vigor and strength, so shall I see enjoyment.
Rain down your dewy treasures o'er our path.
Like loving mothers, pour on us your blessing,
Make us partakers of your sacred essence.
We come to you for cleansing from all guilt,
Cause us to be productive, make us prosper.

*—Rig-Veda X.9*

## January 13

> Endurance, cleanliness,
>     strength, purity
> Will keep our lives straight
> Our actions only for a good
>     purpose.
> Our words will be truth.
> Only honesty shall come from
>     our interaction
> With all things.

> *—From the Lakota Sioux*
> *Sweat Lodge ceremony*

## January 14

*French missionary*
*surgeon Albert Schweitzer*
*is born in 1875*

> Hear our humble prayer, O God,
> for our friends the animals,
> especially for animals who are
> suffering; for any that are
> hunted or lost or deserted or
> frightened or hungry; for all
> that must be put to death. We
> entreat for them all Thy mercy
> and pity, and for those who

deal with them we ask a heart
of compassion and gentle hands
and kindly words. Make us,
ourselves, to be true friends to
animals and so to share the
blessings of the merciful.

*—Albert Schweitzer*

**January 15**
*Civil-rights leader*
*Martin Luther King, Jr.*
*is born in 1929*

> We should never forget that everything Adolf Hitler
> did in Germany was "legal" and everything the
> Hungarian freedom fighters did in Hungary was
> "illegal."

*—Martin Luther King, Jr.*

**January 16**

Empower me
    to be a bold participant,
    rather than a timid saint in waiting,
    in the difficult ordinariness of now;
    to exercise the authority of honesty,

rather than to defer to power,
or deceive to get it;
to influence someone for justice,
rather than impress anyone for gain;
and, by grace, to find treasures
of joy, or friendship, of peace
hidden in the fields of the daily
you give me to plow.

—*Ted Loder*

20

## January 17

Life has meaning only in the struggles.
Triumph or defeat is in the hands of the Gods.
So let us celebrate the struggles.

—*Swahili warrior song*

## January 18

God grant me the serenity to accept the things I
    cannot change;
courage to change the things I can;
and wisdom to know the difference.

Living one day at a time;
Enjoying one moment at a time;
Accepting hardships as the pathway to peace;
Taking this sinful world as it is, not as I would have it;
Trusting that you will make all things right if I
    surrender to your will;
That I may be reasonably happy in this life
And supremely happy with you forever in the next.

    —*Attributed to Reinhold Niebuhr*

## January 19

Lead us from death to life,
from falsehood to truth.
Lead us from despair to hope,
from fear to trust.
Let peace fill our hearts,
our world, our universe.
Let us dream together,
pray together,
work together,
to build one world
of peace and justice for all.

    —*Anonymous*

**January 20**

If you wish only to be healed,
you heal.
Your single purpose makes this possible.
But if you are afraid of healing,
then it cannot come through you.
The only thing that is required for a healing
is lack of fear.
The fearful are not healed,
and cannot heal.
This does not mean the conflict
must be gone forever from your mind to heal.
For if it were,
there were no need for healing then.
But it does mean, if only for an instant,
you love without attack.
An instant is sufficient.
Miracles wait not on time.

—*From A Course in Miracles*
*(Text, page 535)*

## January 21

> O my mother Nut,
> Stretch your wings over me,
> Let me become like the imperishable stars,
> Like the indefatigable stars—
> May Nut extend her arms over me
> And her name of
> "She who extends her arms,
> Chases away the shadows,
> And makes the Light shine
> everywhere."

> —*From an inscription on a*
> *coffin lid in the Louvre*

## January 22

And could you keep your heart in wonder at the daily miracles of life, your pain would not seem less wondrous than your joy.

> —*Kahlil Gibran*

## January 23

*In 1849, Elizabeth Blackwell,*
*the first recognized female*
*doctor, graduates from medical*
*school in New York*

May I escape
the shame, inadequacy, self-judgment and self-doubt
my training has taught me.

May I trust
that my love is as needed as my knowledge.

May I remember
in me
the limitations of everyman.

May I be open
to know my darkness and true to what light I have.

May I be used
as a blessing and a friend to life.

> —*Rachel Naomi Remen, M.D.,*
> *"Hippocratic Oath"*

## January 24

*Prayer before going to the Cancer Clinic for my first radiation treatment:*

Dear Sophia, go with me. Please know that I am not taking my body into this holocaust without immense anguish. I would not injure any part of your earth in any way if I could help it—especially my own body. I still believe we might heal her together. But medical science says it can give me a 98 percent chance of life after cancer. I do not believe I am to die yet. And, for this reason, I am doing this horrendous thing.

Please be with me. Please be my shield. Shield out all the *radiation* that is unnecessary to my healing; keep me open to the *radiance* that will make me whole. Keep me open to what is creative, closed to what is destructive. Into thy loving arms I commend my spirit.

Be very close to me every minute. Keep me in touch with process. Let me act spontaneously. Tell me if I should stop. Oh, let me not be trapped in a conventional procedure that lasts five times a week for five weeks with a 48 hour holocaust at the end. Dear Sophia, let me act out of your courage, out of your wisdom, in every spontaneous moment of every spontaneous day.

I love your Earth, my earth in which I live, move,
and have my Being. I love you. Into thy hands I commend my bodysoul. She is frightened. Please help me
to love her into knowing this is for her continuing life.
This is not instinct. This is not nature. No, this is science working with nature to open new possibilities.

Dear Sophia, be with us, I pray.

—*Marion Woodman*
*8 a.m., January 24, 1994*

## January 25

May suffering ones be suffering free
And the fear struck fearless be.
May the grieving shed all grief—
And the sick find health relief.

—*Zen chant*

## January 26

Last night, as I was sleeping,
I dreamt—marvellous error!—
that I had a beehive
here inside my heart.

And the golden bees
were making white combs
and sweet honey
from my old failures.

> —*Antonio Machado,*
> *"Times Alone"*
> *Translated by Robert Bly*

**January 27**

The Lord is my shepherd, I shall not want. He maketh
me to lie down in green pastures. He leadeth me
beside the still waters. He restoreth my soul. He
leadeth me in the paths of righteousness for His
name's sake. Yea, though I walk through the valley of
the shadow of death, I will fear no evil; for thou art
with me; thy rod and thy staff, they comfort me. Thou
preparest a table before me in the presence of mine
enemies; thou anointest my head with oil; my cup
runneth over. Surely goodness and mercy shall follow
me all the days of my life; and I will dwell in the
house of the Lord forever.

> —*Psalm 23:1*

**January 28**

*Irish poet William Butler
Yeats dies in 1939*

> I am content to follow to its source
> Every event in action or in thought;
> Measure the lot; forgive myself the lot!
> When such as I cast out remorse
> So great a sweetness flows into the breast
> We must laugh and we must sing,
> We are blest by everything
> Everything we look upon is blest.

> —*W.B. Yeats*

**January 29**

In the middle of winter the buds prepare for spring.
Thank you God for unceasing life.

The dull, brown stalks of spent hydrangeas mirror my
spent spirit. Yet green and blue and pink colors dance
in my mind's eye for the spring within and without
about to come.

I feel your presence in pealing cathedral bells, in
insistent cawing crows, in intricate yellow petals of
January forsythia, in new growth heralding coming
spring.

Thank You God for hope.

—*Marian Wright Edelman*

## January 30

Come, come, whoever you are,
Wanderer, worshipper, lover of leaving—
    it doesn't matter,
Ours is not a caravan of despair.
Come, even if you have broken your vows a
    hundred times
Come, come again, come.

—*Rumi*
*Translated by A. J. Arberry*

29

## January 31

*In 1876, all Native*
*Americans are ordered to*
*move into reservations*

Teach your children
what we have taught our children—
that the earth is our mother.
Whatever befalls the earth
befalls the sons and daughters of the earth.
If men spit upon the ground,
they spit upon themselves.

This we know.
The earth does not belong to us;
we belong to the earth.
This we know.
All things are connected
like the blood which unites one family.
All things are connected.

Whatever befalls the earth
befalls the sons and daughters of the earth.
We did not weave the web of life;
We are merely a strand in it.
Whatever we do to the web,
we do to ourselves . . . .

—*Chief Seattle*

## February 1
*St. Brigid's Day,*
*Ireland*

This morning, as I kindle the fire upon my hearth, I pray that the flame of God's love may burn in my heart, and the hearts of all I meet today.

I pray that no envy and malice, no hatred or fear, may smother the flame.

I pray that indifference and apathy, contempt and pride, may not pour like cold water on the fire.

Instead, may the spark of God's love light the love in my heart, that it may burn brightly through the day.

And may I warm those that are lonely, whose hearts are cold and lifeless, so that all may know the comfort of God's love.

*—Traditional Celtic prayer*

### February 2

*Candlemas*

May our eyes remain open even in the face of tragedy.
May we not become disheartened.
May we find in the dissolution
    of our apathy and denial,
    the cup of the broken heart.
May we discover the gift of the fire burning
    in the inner chamber of our being—
    burning great and bright enough
    to transform any poison.
May we offer the power of our sorrow to the service
    of something greater than ourselves.
May our guilt not rise up to form
    yet another defensive wall.
May the suffering purify and not paralyze us.
May we endure; may sorrow bond us and not
    separate us.

May we realize the greatness of our sorrow
    and not run from its touch or its flame.
May clarity be our ally and wisdom our support.
May our wrath be cleansing, cutting through
    the confusion of denial and greed.
May we not be afraid to see or speak our truth.
May the bleakness of the wasteland be dispelled.
May the soul's journey be revealed
    and the true hunger fed.
May we be forgiven for what we have forgotten
    and blessed with the remembrance
    of who we really are.

*—The Terma Collective*

### February 3

Wash me from all that I think I am:
my struggles, my stands, my cherished opinions,
my soaring dreams and deadening fears.
Leave me only Your purity and Your peace.

Wipe away the masks of judgment
I have placed on Your children.
Show me the faces made in Your likeness,
that I may see my own as well.

Brush aside all shrines to the future,
all altars to the past.

Give me Your golden present,
a Home in You, unmovable and eternal.

Still all voices within me.
Fill me with the hush of Your peace.
Now You are my thoughts, my purpose, and my way.
All I need and all I am is You.

—*Hugh Prather*

**February 4**

May I be peaceful, happy, and light in body and in
mind.
May I be safe and free from accidents.
May I be free from anger, unwholesome states of
mind, fear, and worries.
May I know how to look at myself with the eyes of
understanding and love.
May I be able to recognize and touch the seeds of joy
and happiness in myself.
May I learn how to nourish myself with joy each day.
May I be able to live fresh, solid, and free.
May I not fall into the state of indifference
or be caught in the extremes of attachment and
aversion.

May you be peaceful, happy, and light in body and
mind.

May you be safe and free from accidents.

May you be free from anger, unwholesome states of
    mind, fear and worries.

May you know how to look at yourself with the eyes
    of understanding and love.

May you be able to recognize and touch the seeds of
    joy and happiness in yourself.

May you learn how to nourish yourself with joy each
    day.

May you be able to live fresh, solid, and free.

May you not fall into the state of indifference
    or be caught in the extremes of attachment and
    aversion.

May all beings be peaceful, happy, and light in body
    and mind.

May all beings be safe and free from accidents.

May all beings be free from anger, unwholesome
    states of mind, fear, and worries.

May all beings know how to look at themselves with
    the eyes of understanding and love.

May all beings be able to recognize and touch the
    seeds of joy and happiness in themselves.

May all beings learn how to nourish themselves with
    joy each day.

May all beings be able to live fresh, solid, and free.

May all beings not fall into the state of indifference
or caught in the extremes of attachment and
aversion.

*—Thich Nhat Hanh*

### February 5

Releasing the separate one
is a difficult knot.
Finding yourself is something
only you can do.
Imagine yourself coming back
10 years from today
Through time, to help you
where you must now be.

*—Jim Cohn*

### February 6

I reverently speak in the presence of the Great Parent
God: I pray that this day, the whole day, as a child of
God, I may not be taken hold of by my own desire, but
show forth the divine glory by living a life of creative-
ness, which shows forth the true individual.

*—Shinto, date unknown*

## February 7

Hear our humble prayer, O God, for our friends the animals, thy creatures. We pray especially for all that are suffering in any way; for the overworked and underfed, the hunted, lost or hungry; for all in captivity or ill-treated, and for those who must be put to death.

We entreat for them Thy mercy and pity; and for those who deal with them we ask a heart of compassion, gentle hands and kindly words.

Make us all to be true friends to animals.

*—Christian, date unknown*

## February 8

Grandfather,
Look at our brokenness.

We know that in all creation
Only the human family
Has strayed from the Sacred Way.

We know that we are the ones
Who are divided
And we are the ones
Who must come back together
To walk in the Sacred Way.

36

Grandfather,
Sacred One,
Teach us love, compassion, and honor
That we may heal the earth
And heal each other.

—*Ojibway prayer*

## February 9

Healing does not come
from anyone else.
You must accept guidance
from within.

—*From A Course in Miracles
(Text, page 134)*

## February 10

Let us be united;
Let us speak in harmony;
Let our minds apprehend alike.
Common be our prayer;
Common be the end of our assembly;
Common be our resolution;
Common be our deliberations.
Alike be our feelings;

Unified be our hearts;
Common be our intentions;
Perfect be our unity.

—*The Rig-Veda*

### February 11

*In 1858, St. Bernadette
has her vision of the
Virgin Mary at Lourdes*

Lay your hands gently upon us,
let their touch render your peace,
let them bring your forgiveness and healing.
Lay your hands, gently lay your hands.

You were sent to free the broken-hearted,
You were sent to give sight to the blind,
You desire to heal all our illness.
Lay your hands, gently lay your hands.

Lord, we come to you through one another.
Lord, we come to you in all our need.
Lord, we come to you seeking wholeness.
Lay your hands, gently lay your hands.

—*Rita J. Donovan*
*St. Bernadette Chapel, Lourdes, France*

**February 12**
*In 1809, U.S.*
*President Abraham*
*Lincoln is born*

> With malice toward none, with charity for all, with
> firmness in the right, as God gives us to see the right,
> let us...achieve and cherish a just and lasting peace
> among ourselves, and with all nations.

> > —*Abraham Lincoln,*
> > *Second Inaugural Address*

**February 13**

> Every being that lives, grows.
> Each will grow despite harsh
> conditions and beautify its
> surroundings.

> Like a tundra bloom,
> the most striking and beautiful
> flower is the one that blossoms
> despite frigid, brutal conditions.

> > —*Judith Garrett Garrison*
> > *and Scott Sheperd*

## February 14

*St. Valentine's Day*

> Fill my heart with Love,
> that my every teardrop may become a star.

> —*Hazrat Inayat Khan*

## February 15

When sorrow comes, let us accept it simply, as a part of life. Let the heart be open to pain; let it be stretched by it. All the evidence we have says that this is the better way. An open heart never grows bitter. Or if it does, it cannot remain so. In the desolate hour, there is an outcry; a clenching of the hands upon emptiness; a burning pain of bereavement; a weary ache of loss. But anguish, like ecstasy, is not forever. There comes a gentleness, a returning quietness, a restoring stillness. This, too, is a door to life. Here, also, is a deepening of meaning—and it can lead to dedication; a going forward to the triumph of the soul, the conquering of the wilderness. And in the process will come a deepening inward knowledge that in the final reckoning, all is well.

> —*A. Powell Davies*

## February 16

Thy name is my healing, O my God, and remembrance
of Thee is my remedy. Nearness to Thee is my hope,
and love for Thee is my companion. Thy mercy to me
is my healing and my succor in both this world and the
world to come. Thou, verily, art the All-Bountiful, the
All-Knowing, the All-Wise.

—*Baha'u'llah*

## February 17

May we learn to open in love
so all the doors and windows
of our bodies swing wide
on their rusty hinges.

May we learn to give ourselves with both hands,
to lift each other on our shoulders,
to carry one another along.

May holiness move in us
so we pay attention to its small voice
and honor its light in each other.

—*Dawna Markova*

## February 18

O Lord, I place myself in your hands and dedicate
myself to you.

I pledge myself to do your will in all things—

To love the Lord God with all my heart, all my soul,
all my strength.

Not to kill, not to steal, not to covet, not to bear false
witness, to honor all persons.

Not to do to another what I should not want done to
myself.

To chastise the body. Not to seek after pleasures. To
love fasting. To relieve the poor.

To clothe the naked. To visit the sick. To bury the
dead.

To help in trouble. To console the sorrowing.

To hold myself aloof from worldly ways.

To prefer nothing to the love of Christ.

Not to give way to anger. Not to foster a desire for
revenge.

Not to entertain deceit in the heart. Not to make a
false peace.

Not to forsake charity.

Not to swear, lest I swear falsely.

To speak the truth with heart and tongue

Not to return evil for evil.

To do no injury, indeed, even to bear patiently any
injury done to me.

To love my enemies. Not to curse those who curse me
      but rather to bless them.

To bear persecution for justice's sake.

Not to be proud.

Not to be given to intoxicating drink. Not to be an
      overeater.

Not to be lazy. Not to be slothful.

Not to be a murmurer. Not to be a detractor.

To put my trust in God.

To refer the good I see in myself to God.

To refer any evil I see in myself to myself.

To fear the day of judgment. To be in dread of hell.

To desire eternal life with spiritual longing.

To keep death before my eyes daily.

To keep constant watch over my actions.

To remember that God sees me everywhere.

To call upon Christ for defense against evil thoughts
      that arise in my heart.

To guard my tongue against wicked speech.

To avoid much speaking. To avoid idle talk.

Not to seek to appear clever.

To read only what is good to read.

To pray often.

To ask forgiveness daily for my sins, and to seek ways
      to amend my life.

To obey my superiors in all things rightful.

Not to desire to be thought holy, but to seek holiness.

To fulfill the commandments of God by good works.

To love chastity. To hate no one. Not be jealous or
envious of anyone.

Not to love strife. Not to love pride.

To honor the aged. To pray for my enemies.

To make peace after a quarrel, before the setting of the
sun.

Never to despair of your mercy, O God of Mercy.

—*Saint Benedict*

### February 19

To ignore God as of little use in sickness is a mistake.
Instead of thrusting Him aside in times of bodily trouble, and waiting for the hour of strength in which to
acknowledge Him, we should learn that He can do all
things for us in sickness as in health.

—*Mary Baker Eddy,*
*Science and Health with Key to*
*the Scriptures*

### February 20

How would it be
if just for today
we thought less about contests and rivalries,

profits and politics,
winners and sinners,
and more about
helping and giving,
mending and blending,
reaching out
and pitching in?

How would it be?

—*Anonymous*

**February 21**

The whole course of things goes to teach us faith.
We need only obey. There is guidance for each of us,
and by lowly listening we shall hear the right word....
Place yourself in the middle of the stream of power and
wisdom which flows into you as life, place yourself in
the full center of that flood, then you are without effort
impelled to truth, to right, and a perfect contentment.

—*Ralph Waldo Emerson*

## February 22

*In 1940, five-year-old*
*Tenzin Gyatso is recognized*
*as the 14th Dalai Lama in Tibet*

Please pacify the uninterrupted miseries
and unbearable fears,
such as famines and sicknesses,
that torment powerless beings
completely oppressed by inexhaustible
and violent evils,
and henceforth lead us from suffering states
and place us in an ocean of happiness and joy.

Those who, maddened by the demons of delusion,
commit violent negative actions
that destroy both themselves and others,
should be the object of our compassion.
May the hosts of undisciplined beings
fully gain the eye that knows
what to abandon and practice,
and be granted a wealth
of loving kindness and friendliness.

Through the force of dependent-arising,
which by nature is profound
and empty of appearances,
the force of the Words of Truth,
the power of the kindness of the Three Jewels

and the true power of non-deceptive actions
and their effects;
may my prayer of truth
be accomplished quickly and without hindrance.

—*His Holiness*
*The Fourteenth Dalai Lama*

## February 23

From joy I came,
For joy I live,
And in Thy sacred joy
I shall melt again.

—*Yogananda,*
*Whispers from Eternity*

## February 24

We may wonder whom can I love and serve?
Where is the face of God to whom I can pray?
The answer is simple. That naked one. That lonely
one. That unwanted one is my brother and my sister.
If we have no peace, it is because we have forgotten
that we belong to each other.

—*Mother Teresa*

**February 25**
*Ash Wednesday*
*(date varies)*

> But I say to you that listen, Love your enemies, do
> good to those who hate you, bless those who curse
> you, pray for those who abuse you.
>
> If anyone strikes you on the cheek, offer the other
> also; and from anyone who takes away your coat do not
> withhold even your shirt.
>
> —*Luke 6:27*

**February 26**

> "Jacob, where do you find the strength to carry
> on in life?"
>
> "Life is often heavy only because we attempt to
> carry it," said Jacob. "But, I do find a strength in the
> ashes."
>
> "In the ashes?" asked Mr. Gold.
>
> "Yes," said Jacob, with a confirmation that seemed
> to have traveled a great distance.
>
> "You see, Mr. Gold, each of us is alone. Each of us
> is in the great darkness of our ignorance. And, each of
> us is on a journey.
>
> "In the process of our journey, we must bend to
> build a fire for light, and warmth, and food.

"But when our fingers tear at the ground, hoping to find the coals of another's fire, what we often find are the ashes.

"And, in these ashes, which will not give us light or warmth, there may be sadness, but there is also testimony.

"Because these ashes tell us that somebody else has been in the night, somebody else has bent to build a fire, and somebody else has carried on.

"And that can be enough, sometimes."

—*Noah benShea*

**February 27**

When healing is the target
Illness is the bow.
What is a bow but a device for the transfer of energy?
Likewise an illness.

Properly used, an illness turns an outward focus
     inward,
Sends energy to where it's needed most.
Transforms fears into strength
Arrogance into humility
Compulsion to caring
Cynicism to compassion
Brings balance to imbalance.

*The release of pain over-long denied.*

Worldly medicine does the opposite.
It requires the patient to look outside herself
To give her power to another
To maintain control
To invade the body
To deny the spirit.

One who embraces illness as well as health
Embraces the whole of life.
She can offer life.
Because she receives life.

—*Haven Treviño*

### February 28

May people be well, may they be well,
Male, female, male, female,
Goats, cattle, boys and girls;
May they multiply themselves.
Bad luck go away from us . . .

—*An elder of the Kithuri clan,
the Meru of Kenya*

**February 29**

*Leap Year Day*

> Oh Great Spirit of Surprise,
>> dazzle us with a day full of amazing embraces,
>>> capricious, uncalculated caring,
>>> great hearts, kind souls and doers of
>>>> good deeds.

> —*Molly Fumia*

**March 1**

> Dewdrop, let me cleanse
> in your brief
> sweet waters...
> These dark hands of life

> —*Basho*

**March 2**

*English poet and author*
*D.H. Lawrence dies in 1930*

> I am not a mechanism, an assembly of various sections.
> And it is not because the mechanism is working
> wrongly,
>> that I am ill.
> I am ill because of wounds to the soul,
>> to the deep emotional self

and the wounds to the soul take a long, long time,
    only time can help
and patience, and a certain difficult repentance,
long, difficult repentance, realisation of life's mistake,
and the
    freeing oneself
from the endless repetition of the mistake

which mankind at large has chosen to sanctify.

    —*D.H. Lawrence*

## March 3

All things in this creation exist within you, and all
things in you exist in creation; there is no border
between you and the closest things, and there is no
distance between you and the farthest things, and all
things, from the lowest to the loftiest, from the smallest
to the greatest, are within you as equal things. In one
atom are found all the elements of the earth; in one
motion of the mind are found the motions of all the
laws of existence; in one drop of water are found the
secrets of all the endless oceans; in one aspect of *you* are
found all the aspects of *existence* ... [Thus] "Your life has
no end, and you shall live forevermore."

    —*Kahlil Gibran*

**March 4**

May the Wind breathe healing upon us,
    prolong our life-span,
and fill our hearts with comfort!

You are our father, O Wind,
    our friend and our brother.
Give us life that we may live.

From that immortal treasure, O Lord,
    which is hidden in your abode,
impart to us that we may live.

> —*The Vedas*
> *Translated by Raimundo Panniker*

**March 5**

There are moments when wellness escapes us,
moments when pain and suffering
are not dim possibilities
but all too agonizing realities.
At such moments we must open ourselves to healing.

Much we can do for ourselves;
and what we can do
we must do—

healing,
no less than illness,
is participatory.

But even when we do all we can do
there is,
often,
still much left to be done.
And so we turn as well to our healers
seeking their skill to aid in our struggle for wellness.

But even when they do all they can do
there is,
often,
still much left to be done.
And so we turn to Life,
to the vast Power of Being that animates the universe
as the ocean animates the wave,
seeking to let go of that which blocks our healing.

May those
whose lives are gripped in the palm of suffering
open
even now
to the Wonder of Life.
May they let go of the hurt
and Meet the True Self beyond pain,
the Uncarved Block
that is our joyous Unity with Holiness.

May they discover through pain and torment
the strength to live with grace and humor.
May they discover through doubt and anguish
the strength to live with dignity and holiness.
May they discover through suffering and fear
the strength to move toward healing.

—*Rabbi Rami M. Shapiro*

**March 6**

As you close your eyes,
sink into stillness.
Let these periods of rest and respite
reassure your mind
that all its frantic fantasies
were but the dreams of fever
that has passed away.
Let it be still
and thankfully accept its healing.
No more fearful dreams will come,
now that you rest in God.

—*From A Course in Miracles*
*(Workbook, page 193)*

**March 7**

> Live in the present,
> Do all the things that need to be done.
> Do all the good you can each day.
> The future will unfold.

> —*Peace Pilgrim*

**March 8**

> Let us take care of the children,
> for they have a long way to go.

> Let us take care of the elders,
> for they have come a long way.

> Let us take care of those in between,
> for they are doing the work.

> —*African prayer*

**March 9**

> I am the child of the universe.
> She puts her almighty protection around me.
> I am free from accidents, death, sickness.
> I am now shining with golden light from top to toe.
> I am her chosen protected child, and she is my shield.

The winds shall aid my progress.
Water shall cleanse me from fear,
Fire will purify my doubts,
And the earth shall nourish me to health.
All is well, all is well, all is well.

—*Zsuzsanna E. Budapest*

## March 10

Knowing how deeply our lives intertwine,
    We vow not to kill.
Knowing how deeply our lives intertwine,
    We vow to not take what is not given.
Knowing how deeply our lives intertwine,
    We vow to not engage in abusive relationships.
Knowing how deeply our lives intertwine,
    We vow to not speak falsely or deceptively.
Knowing how deeply our lives intertwine,
    We vow to not harm self or others through
    poisonous thought or substance.
Knowing how deeply our lives intertwine,
    We vow to not dwell on past errors.
Knowing how deeply our lives intertwine,
    We vow to not speak of self separate from
    others.
Knowing how deeply our lives intertwine,
    We vow to not possess any thing or form of life
    selfishly.

Knowing how deeply our lives intertwine,
>    We vow to not harbor ill will toward any plant,
>    animal, or human being.

Knowing how deeply our lives intertwine,
>    We vow to not abuse the great truth of the
>    Three Treasures.

>    —*Stephanie Kaza,*
>    *Green Gulch Farm*

### March 11

Have mercy on me, O Beneficent One, I was angered
for I had no shoes: then I met a man who had no feet.

>    —*Chinese saying*

### March 12

Thou Infinite One, it is Thy grace,
the highest opportunity for humanity
that we can sit and think and be together
>    to praise thee, O Lord.
O creative consciousness, O cosmos, moment of
>    positive existence, positive relationship,
>    positive love and brotherhood,
dedicated unto this, the highest reward on this
>    planet for the individual being,

and You are the one who granted it.
Our gratitude for this,
and may your blessings shower upon us
to make us healthy, happy, and holy
and may we live in a raised consciousness of
universal consciousness of love, peace, and harmony.
Give us the power to exalt thee.
Give us the power to be thy channel.

—*Yogi Bhajan*

## March 13

House made of dawn.
House made of evening light.
House made of the dark cloud.
House made of male rain.
House made of dark mist.
House made of female rain.
House made of pollen.
House made of grasshoppers.

Dark cloud is at the door.
The trail out of it is dark cloud.
The zigzag lightning stands high upon it.
An offering I make.
Restore my feet for me.
Restore my legs for me.
Restore my body for me.

Restore my mind for me.
Restore my voice for me.
This very day take out your spell for me.

Happily I recover.
Happily my interior becomes cool.
Happily I go forth.
My interior feeling cool, may I walk.
No longer sore, may I walk.
Impervious to pain, may I walk.
With lively feelings may I walk.
As it used to be long ago, may I walk.

Happily may I walk.
Happily, with abundant dark clouds, may I walk.
Happily, with abundant showers, may I walk.
Happily, with abundant plants, may I walk.
Happily, on a trail of pollen, may I walk.
Happily may I walk.
Being as it used to be long ago, may I walk.

May it be beautiful before me.
May it be beautiful behind me.
May it be beautiful below me.
May it be beautiful above me.
May it be beautiful all around me.
In beauty it is finished.
In beauty it is finished.

*—Navaho chant*

## March 14

From the cowardice that shrinks from new truth,
From the laziness that is content with half-truths,
From the arrogance that thinks it knows all truth,
O God of Truth, deliver us.

*—An ancient scholar*

## March 15

It is the wind and the rain, O God, the cold and the
storm that make this earth of Thine to blossom and
bear its fruit. So in our lives it is storm and stress and
hurt and suffering that make real men and women
bring the world's work to its highest perfection. Let us
learn then in these growing years to respect the harder
sterner aspects of life together with its joy and laughter,
and to weave them all into the great web which hangs
holy to the Lord.

*—W.E.B. Du Bois*

## March 16

> May the passions of lust, anger, greed, pride and attachment depart from me. O Lord, I come to seek Thy shelter: Bless me with thy grace.

> —*Sacred song of the Sikhs*

## March 17

*Saint Patrick's Day*

> I take for my sureties:
>
> The power of God to guide me,
> The might of God to uphold me,
> The wisdom of God to teach me,
> The eye of God to watch over me,
> The ear of God to hear me,
> The word of God to give me speech,
> The hand of God to protect me,
> The way of God to go before me,
> The shield of God to shelter me...
>
> Christ be with me, Christ before me,
> Christ behind me, Christ within me,
> Christ beneath me, Christ above me,
> Christ at my right, Christ at my left,
> Christ in the heart of every man who thinks of me,
> Christ in the mouth of every man who speaks to me,

Christ in every eye that sees me,
Christ in every ear that hears me.

—*St. Patrick*

## March 18

I want what is left:
The tea leaves, the soiled images on cards,
The gasp of words as meaning slips away,
The rinds of the alphabet,
The chewed poems of prisoners,
The bones and the skeletons,
The secretions, the shattered sperm,
The spilled blood,
Broken ova, the phlegm and the cough.

It has always been women's work to prepare the
    corpse.

But, I will not make a corpse from these elements,
I will make a child.
I will make you such a rose of a child,
A rose of a child held in the crook
Of the dark hand of a dead branch,
I will make you a child shining
Like an angel from these elements of dark,
And the child will sing.

This is what we have
This is what we have to work with.

So give them to me,
First, your dead, moldering
In the dreadful heat of your deserted cities,
Then, give me the iron birds in the sky,
With their demented warbling,
Last, I want your radiant soil
With its eternal shimmer,
Give me everything mangled and bruised,
And I will make a light of it to make you weep,
And we will have rain,
And begin again.

—*Deena Metzger,*
*"Leavings"*
*For Sister Cao ngor Phuong*

**March 19**

This is the way the rhythm moves. The fall of the year
comes, then winter with its trees stripped of leaf and
bud; cold winds ruthless in bitterness and sting. One
day there is sleet and ice; in the silence of the night-
time the snow falls soundlessly—all this until at last the
cold seems endless and all there is seems to be shadowy
and foreboding. The earth is weary and heavy. Then

64

something stirs—a strange new vitality pulses through everything. One can feel the pressure of some vast energy pushing, always pushing through dead branches, slumbering roots—life surges everywhere within and without. Spring has come. The day usurps the night view.

Is there any wonder that deeper than idea and concept is the insistent conviction that the night can never stay, that winter is ever moving toward the spring? Thus, when a man sees the lights go out one by one, when he sees the end of his days marked by death—his death—he *senses,* rather than knows, that even the night into which he is entering will be followed by day. It remains for religion to give this ancient wisdom phrase and symbol. For millions of men and women in many climes this phrase and this symbol are forever one with Jesus, the Prophet from Galilee. When the preacher says as a part of the last rites, "I am the Resurrection and the Life, . . ." he is reminding us all of the ancient wisdom: "Upon the night view of the world, a day view must follow."

—*Howard Thurman*

SPRING

## March 20
*Vernal Equinox*

Everywhere is the green of new growth,
The amazing sight of the renewal of the earth.
We watch the grass once again emerging from the
     ground.
We notice the bright green atop the dark green on the
     pine, the fir, the hemlock, the spruce, the cedar.
The alder is already in leaf.
The old plum trees still blossom, leaf and give forth
     fruit.
The locust is late as always.
Everywhere and always the song of birds . . . bees
     raiding the orchard, racoon prowling at
     nightfall, the earthworm tunneling the garden,
     chickens and rabbits pecking and nibbling, the
     goats tugging to reach new delights . . . all are the
     ubiquitous energies of life.

O Lord,
May we today be touched by grace, fascinated and
     moved by this your creation, energized by the
     power of new growth at work in your world.
May we move beyond viewing this life only through a
     frame, but
         touch it and be touched by it,
         know it and be known by it,
         love it and be loved by it.

68

May our bodies, our minds, our spirits, learn a new
     rhythm paced by the rhythmic pulse of the
     whole created order.
May spring come to us, be in us, and recreate life in
     us.
May we forge a new friendship with the natural
     world and discover a new affinity with beauty,
     with life, and with the Cosmic Christ in whom
     all things were created in heaven and on earth,
     visible or invisible, whether thrones or
     dominions or principalities or authorities . . . for
     all things were created through him and for
     him.
In his name.
Amen.

—*Chinook Psalter*

**March 21**

*German composer*
*Johann Sebastian*
*Bach is born in 1685*

At the far end of the wooden bridge is a small
lake in an old granite quarry. Two white swans swim in
utter peace. Their long necks curl into feathered question marks. Silently, they glide across the still water.

When the morning sun crests the distant treetops,
loudspeakers attached to the soaring stone walls switch

on and into the canyon rumbles Bach's *Toccata and Fugue*. I sit on a carved bench at the edge of the water, watching the play of light on the lake, listening to the deep drone that swells the air. As the organ music fades, it's followed languorously by the *Brandenburg Concertos*. Into the sheer blue sky rises the sounds of joyously conversing violins.

Suddenly the spell is split in two by the shrill sawmill cries of a chainsaw from the forest at the edge of the park. Metal teeth gnash the air. Motors growl on and off. White-flashing blades bite into ancient bark. The forest moans as great branches crash to the ground.

An unseen hand turns up the volume of the music, as if to drown out the slashing sounds. The strange syncopation of falling trees and soaring violins jolts a sidelong memory out of me. A dusty trunk in the attic of memory opens wide and I recall a legend.

During one brutal winter in Germany a sudden frost destroyed all the apple trees in Bach's grove but one. Desperate to save his last tree, he ventured out into the stricken field with the only protection he could think of, the manuscript pages of his Brandenburg concertos. With those parchment bandages, he tenderly wrapped the bark of the dying tree, and saved it from the killing frost.

Out in the middle of the stilled lake, the swans twitch violently to each snarl of the chainsaws. The last

movement of the sixth concerto fades away, leaving
only the grinding of sawblades, and the alertness of two
white swans, who wait for the next wave of healing
music.

—*Phil Cousineau*
*"Bach in Brazil"*

## March 22

*German philosopher*
*Johann Wolfgang von Goethe*
*dies in 1832.*

*His last words were reported*
*to be "More light!"*

The way you see people is the way you treat them
and the way you treat them is what they become.

—*Johann W. von Goethe*

## March 23

The light of God surrounds me;
The love of God enfolds me;
The power of God protects me;
The presence of God watches over me.
Wherever I am, God is.

—*James Dillet Freeman*

## March 24

Refuse to fall down.
If you cannot refuse to fall down,
refuse to stay down.
If you cannot refuse to stay down,
lift your heart toward heaven,
and like a hungry beggar,
ask that it be filled,
and it will be filled.
You may be pushed down.
You may be kept from rising.
But no one can keep you
from lifting your heart
toward heaven—
only you.
It is in the middle of misery
that so much becomes clear.
The one who says nothing good
came of this,
is not yet listening.

> —*Clarissa Pinkola Estés, Ph.D.,*
> *"Refuse to Fall Down"*

**March 25**

Beloved God,

Show me the truth about this.

I now surrender all fears, doubts, and judgments, and
invite the light of perfect consciousness to
illuminate my path.

Pure love is present here and now, as God lives in
every person I meet.

I send love and appreciation to all my associates,
knowing with perfect confidence that he or she
is guided by the same Great Spirit that guides
me.

I am not separate from my brothers and sisters, but
one with them.

I trust that my highest good is unfolding before me,
and I accept the very best that love and life
have to offer.

I am worthy of living in the kingdom of Heaven, even
as I walk the earth. I claim it now.

Thank you, God, for loving me infinitely, and opening
all doors for the highest good of all concerned.

I receive Your love, and magnify it.

And so it is.

—*Alan Cohen*

## March 26

Please bless this wee one, dear God,
And keep her safe from harm
And when she suffers in the night
Let her feel Your loving arms.

She gives such love and joy
To us, on Your earth below,
And we show her care and kindness
In the only ways we know.

She does not speak of pain,
Only curiosity and delight,
And to help her feel her best
We turn her over to Your might.

Please bless this wee one, dear God,
And help her feel better soon.
This our prayer we send to you,
On light of sun, stars, and moon.
Amen.

> —*Lydia Barrett, on behalf of*
> *her pet mouse Niblick (whose ears healed)*

## March 27

Sweet Spirit of Sleep, who brings peace and rest to
weary bodies,

    Empty us of aches and pains,

74

for we struggle as seeds through unyielding
earth.
Bring to us the timeless nature of your presence—
the endless void of our slumber.
Make us aware of the work we can do while in
your time;
Make us to know our dreaming,
where past and future are reconciled.
Come let us honor sleep, that knits up
the raveled sleeve of care, the death of each day's life,
sore labor's bath, balm of hurt minds,
great nature's second course,
chief nourisher in life's feast.

—*Congregation of Abraxas*

## March 28
*Saint Teresa of Avila
is born in 1515*

Let nothing disturb you
nothing frighten you,
all things are passing;
Patient endurance
attains all things:
one whom God possesses
wants nothing
for God alone suffices.

—*Saint Teresa of Avila*

**March 29**

Let there be peace, welfare and righteousness
in every part of the world.

Let confidence and friendship prevail
for the good of east and west
for the good of the needy south
for the good of all humanity.

Let the people inspire their leaders
helping them to seek peace by peaceful means
helping them and urging them
to build a better world
a world with a home for everybody
a world with food and work for everybody
a world with spiritual freedom
for everybody.

Let those who have the power of money
be motivated by selfless compassion.
Let money become a tool
for the good of humankind.

Let those who have power
deal respectfully with the resources of the planet.
Let them respect and maintain
the purity of the air, water, land and subsoil.
Let them co-operate to restore
the ecological soundness of Mother Earth.

Let trees grow up by the billions
around the world.
Let green life invade the deserts.

Let industry serve humanity
and produce waste that serves nature.

Let technology respect
the holiness of Mother Earth.

Let those who control the mass media
contribute to create mutual understanding
contribute to create optimism and confidence.

Let ordinary people
meet by the millions across the borders.
Let them create a universal network
of love and friendship.

Let billions of human beings
co-operate to create a good future
for their children and grandchildren.

Let us survive
In peace and harmony with Mother Earth.

*—Hagen Hasselbalch*

## March 30

You do not have to be good.
You do not have to walk on your knees
for a hundred miles through the desert, repenting.
You only have to let the soft animal of your body
    love what it loves.
Tell me about despair, yours, and I will tell you mine.
Meanwhile the world goes on.
Meanwhile the sun and the clear pebbles of the rain
are moving across the landscapes,
over the prairies and the deep trees,
the mountains and the rivers.
Meanwhile the wild geese, high in the clean blue air,
are heading home again.
Whoever you are, no matter how lonely,
the world offers itself to your imagination,
calls to you like the wild geese, harsh and exciting—
over and over announcing your place
in the family of things.

—*Mary Oliver*

## March 31

When the wind blows
    that is my medicine
When it rains
    that is my medicine

When it hails
    that is my medicine
When it becomes clear after a storm
    that is my medicine

—*Anonymous*

## April 1
*All Fools' Day*

Give me a sense of humor,
Give me the grace to see a joke,
To get some pleasure out of life
And pass it on to other folk.

—*Anonymous*

## April 2

Lord of the springtime, Father of flower, field and fruit,
smile on us in these earnest days when the work is
heavy and the toil wearisome; lift up our hearts, O
God, to the things worthwhile—sunshine and night,
the dripping rain, the song of the birds, books and
music, and the voices of our friends. Lift up our hearts
to these this night and grant us Thy peace. Amen.

—*W.E.B. Du Bois*

**April 3**

> Live in simple faith...
> Just as this
> trusting cherry
> flowers, fades, and falls
>
> —*Issa*

80    **April 4**

> O our Father, the Sky, hear us
>     and make us strong.
> O our Mother the Earth, hear us
>     and give us support.
> O Spirit of the East,
>     send us your Wisdom.
> O Spirit of the South,
>     may we tread your path of life.
> O Spirit of the West,
>     may we always be ready for the long journey.
> O Spirit of the North, purify us
>     with your cleansing winds.
>
> —*Sioux prayer*

**April 5**

When each day
is sacred

when each hour
is sacred

when each instant
is sacred

earth and you
space and you
bearing the sacred
through time

you'll reach
the fields of light.

—*Guillevic*


**April 6**

God, protect us from and keep us from being
        Hypocrites
        Experts
        Attention huggers
        Blamers and complainers
        Snake oil salespeople

Takers and just talkers
Lone Rangers
Excuse makers
Fair weather workers
Braggers
Magic bullet seekers and sellers and
Quitters.
God, send us and help us to be
Righteous warriors
Moral guerrillas
Scut workers
Nitty-gritty doers
Detail tenders
Long-distance runners
Energetic tryers
Risk takers
Sharers
Team players
Organizers and mobilizers and
Servant leaders,
to save our children.

—*Marian Wright Edelman*

## April 7
*World Health Day*

> O Thou in whose great arms
> All the children of earth are embraced,
> Here in thy presence we remember
>     our kinship with all human kind.
>
> We rejoice for those who are in
>     full health and strength,
> Whose ways are ways of pleasantness
>     and peace.
>
> Our hearts reach out toward those
>     whose ways are ways of suffering,
>     of body, mind, or soul.
>
> May it be that thou shalt find us
>     reaching out to them
> Not only with our hearts but with
>     our hands also,
> To help them in the bearing of
>     their burdens,
> To help in the lifting of their
>     burdens.

*—Robert French Leavens*

## April 8

If you have one hour of air
and many hours to go,
you must breathe slowly.

If you have one arm's length
and many things to care for,
you must give freely.

If you have one chance to know God
and many doubts, you must
set your heart on fire.

We are blessed.

Each day is a chance.
We have two arms
Fear wastes air.

>                 —*Mark Nepo,*
>                   *"Freefall"*

## April 9

*The Civil War ends*
*in 1863 when Confederate*
*Gen. Robert E. Lee*
*surrenders to Union*
*Gen. Ulysses S. Grant*

Father! Before thy throne come,
Not in the panoply of war,
With pealing trump, and rolling drum,
And cannon booming loud and far;
Striving in blood to wash out blood,
Through wrong to seek redress for wrong:
For while tho'rt holy, just and good,
The battle is not to the strong;
But in the sacred name of peace,
Of justice, virtue, love and truth,
We pray, and never mean to cease,
Till weak old age and fiery youth
In freedom's cause their voices raise,
And burst the bonds of every slave;
Till, north and south, and east and west,
The wrongs we bear shall be redressed.

—*J.M. Whitfield*
*(African-American abolitionist*
*during the Civil War)*

**April 10**

*The American Society for
the Prevention of Cruelty
to Animals (ASPCA)
is founded in 1886*

O God, source of life and power, Who feedeth the
birds of the heavens, increase our tenderness towards all
the creatures of Thy hand. Help us to refrain from
petty acts of cruelty, or thoughtless deeds of harm to
any living animal. May we care for them at all times,
especially during hard weather, and protect them from
injury so that they learn to trust us as friends. Let our
sympathy grow with knowledge, so that the whole creation may rejoice in Thy presence.

—*Christian,
date unknown*

**April 11**

*Passover
(date varies)*

*To be said while lighting candles:*

We begin by honoring the Light.
We light these candles for our families, our beloveds,
 our friends, for all our relations;

For those who are near and for those from whom
we feel an unwanted distance;
For the newborn, for the elderly, and for all the
wounded children.
May the candles inspire us to use our powers
to heal and not to harm, to help and not to
hinder, to bless and not to curse.
May their radiance pour out upon our hearts, and
spread light into the darkened corners of our world.

—*Adapted from a Passover Haggadah
by Rachel Altman and Mary Jane Ryan*

**April 12**
*Easter
(date varies)*

All powerlessness stems from failure to understand this
point: The key to empowerment, personal and collective, is the understanding that, although darkness stalks
light, the light will always reassert itself. No matter
what is happening, the universe is invested in healing.
Night is followed by morning. Crucifixion is followed
by Resurrection. God always has the final say.

—*Marianne Williamson*

**April 13**

New seed
is faithful.
It roots deepest
in the places
that are
most empty.

> —*Clarissa Pinkola Estés, Ph. D.,*
> *"The Ultimate Faith"*

**April 14**

Just as the soft rains fill the streams,
pour into the rivers and join together in the oceans,
so may the power of every moment of your goodness
flow forth to awaken and heal all beings,
Those here now, those gone before, those yet to come.

By the power of every moment of your goodness
May your heart's wishes be soon fulfilled
as completely shining as the bright full moon,
as magically as by a wish-fulfilling gem.

By the power of every moment of your goodness
May all dangers be averted and all disease be gone.
May no obstacle come across your way.
May you enjoy fulfillment and long life.

For all in whose heart dwells respect,
who follow the wisdom and compassion, of the Way,
May your life prosper in the four blessings
of old age, beauty, happiness and strength.

> —*Traditional Buddhist blessing*
> *and healing chant (version by*
> *Jack Kornfield)*

## April 15

O budded, greening branch!
You stand as firmly rooted in your nobility
As the dawn advances.
Now rejoice and be glad;
Consider us frail ones worthy
To free us from our destructive ways:
Put forth your hand and
Raise us up.

> —*Saint Hildegard of Bingen*

## April 16

We join with the Earth
and with each other,
With our ancestors and
all beings of the future,

to bring new life to the land,
to recreate the human community,
to provide justice and peace,
to remember our children,
to remember who we are...
We join together
as many and diverse expressions
of one loving Mystery,
for the healing of the Earth
and the renewal of all Life.

—*Pat Mathes Cane*

### April 17

You carry the cure within you.
Everything that comes your way is blessed.
The Creator gives you one more day.
Stand on the neck of Fearful Mind.

Do not wait to open your heart.
Let yourself go into the Mystery.
Sometimes the threads have no weave.
The price of not loving yourself is high.

—*Jim Cohn*

**April 18**

Ward off from us, disease and weakness.
By day and night, lovers of sweetness, guard us.

—*Rig-Veda*

(Note: The "lovers of sweetness" are two Vedic gods, the Asvins,
inseparable twins, who are fond of plant-juice liquors)

**April 19**

Fear does not gladden.
Healing does.
Fear always makes exceptions.
Healing never does.
Fear produces dissociation,
because it induces separation.
Healing always produces harmony,
because it proceeds from integration.

—*From A Course in Miracles*
*(Text, page 112)*

## April 20

Life is so generous a giver, but we, judging its gifts by their covering, cast them away as ugly or heavy, or hard. Remove the covering, and you will find beneath it a living splendor, woven of love, by wisdom, with power.

Welcome it, grasp it, and you touch the angel's hand that brings it to you. Everything we call a trial, a sorrow or a duty, believe me, that angel's hand is there; the gift is there, and the wonder of an overshadowing presence. Our joys too: be not content with them as joys. They too conceal diviner gifts.

And so, at this time, I greet you.
Not quite as the world sends greetings, but with profound esteem and with the prayer that for you now and forever, the day breaks, and the shadows flee.

—*Fra Giovanni*

## April 21

You're song,
a wished-for song.

Go through the ear to the center
where sky is, where wind,
where silent knowing.

Put seeds and cover them.
Blades will sprout
where you do your work.

—*Rumi*
*Translated by Coleman Barks*

**April 22**

May we walk with grace
and may the light of the universe
shine upon our path.

—*Anonymous*

**April 23**

Our true home is in the present moment.
To live in the present moment is a miracle.
The miracle is not to walk on water.
The miracle is to walk on the green Earth in the present moment,
to appreciate the peace and beauty that are available now.
Peace is all around us—
in the world and in nature—
and within us—
in our bodies and our spirits.

Once we learn to touch this peace,
we will be healed and transformed.
It is not a matter of faith;
it is a matter of practice.

—*Thich Nhat Hanh*

### April 24

Hear, O Humankind, the prayer of my heart

For are we not one, have we not one desire,
to heal our Mother Earth and bind her wounds
to hear again from dark forests and flashing rivers
the varied ever-changing Song of Creation?

O humankind, are we not all brothers and sisters,
are we not the grandchildren of the Great Mystery?
Do we not all want to love and be loved, to work
and to play, to sing and dance together?

But we live with fear. Fear that is hate, fear
that is mistrust, envy, greed, vanity, fear that is
ambition, competition, aggression, fear that is
loneliness, anger, bitterness, cruelty...and yet,
fear is only twisted love, love turned back on itself,
love that was denied, love that was rejected...
and love...
        Love is life—creation, seed and leaf
and blossom and fruit and seed, love is growth

and search and reach and touch and dance.
Love is nurture and succor and feed and pleasure,
love is pleasuring ourselves pleasuring each other,
love is life believing in itself.
     And life . . .
Life is the Sacred Mystery singing to itself, dancing
to its drum, telling tales, improvising, playing
and we are all that Spirit, our stories all
but one cosmic story that we are love indeed,
that perfect love in me seeks the love in you,
and if our eyes could ever meet without fear
we would recognize each other and rejoice,
for love is life believing in itself.

—*Manitongquat*


**April 25**

God, like a sojourner called forth from your garden, I
abide upon this maternal soil to be a transparent messenger of your peace. Therefore, my will and my life I
entrust into your hands. Mold me as you see fit for
whatever you give me. I am grateful. Whatever you
send me, I accept.

Sustain me only with your wisdom and your love
so that all whom I meet on this journey home may see
through me to you.

—*Craig O'Neill*

## April 26

Iba'che NaNa★, Womb of Creation.
She Who Gave Birth to All Things.
From your dark depths the first spark came into Being.
Your luminous Egg exploded in the midst of eternal
    night,
its joyous dance formed the great lights.

You Who Gave Us Sun and Moon, Earth and Sky,
    Body and Spirit.
Awaken from your sleep, Deep Night.
Lift your eyelids and see our plight.
The children of Earth are in need of your guidance;
they await the feel of your hand.
They roll their eyes in great suspicion,
in anger and fear they strike out.
Their hearts are hard, their hands are trembling.
Amidst the rubble of war, they cry out.

Hear me Great Mother, hear your daughter.
Open your starlit thighs. Draw us back into your vulva.
Mix us, stir us, roll and squeeze;
mold our heads,
pat our behinds.
Change us, every cell and spirit 'til Peace possesses
    our minds.

Blow your perfumed breath upon us,
wash us in the deep blue sea.
Suckle us on milk and honey,
oil us with the balm of love.

Return us then to this green garden,
Oh Beautiful, Generous Mother,
but this time
give us also the wisdom to see your reflection in each
other.

—*Luisah Teish*

(*A Yoruba term of great respect)

## April 27
*U.S. writer and
philosopher Ralph Waldo
Emerson dies in 1882*

Teach me your mood, O patient stars!
Who climb each night the ancient sky,
Leaving on space no shade, no scars,
No trace of age, no fear to die.

—*Ralph Waldo Emerson*

## April 28

As no one desires the slightest suffering
nor ever has enough of happiness,
there is no difference between myself and others,
so let me make others joyfully happy.

May those feeble with cold find warmth,
and may those oppressed with heat be cooled
by the boundless waters that pour forth
from the great clouds of the Bodhisattvas.

May the rains of lava, blazing stones and weapons
from now on become a rain of flowers,
and may all battling with weapons
from now on be a playful exchange of flowers.

May the naked find clothing,
the hungry find food;
may the thirsty find water
and delicious drinks.

May the frightened cease to be afraid
and those bound be freed;
may the powerless find power,
and may people think of benefiting one another.

For as long as space endures
and for as long as living beings remain,

until then may I too abide
to dispel the misery of the world.

—*Santideva*

## April 29
*U.S. composer and pianist*
*Duke Ellington is born in 1899*

Every man prays in his own language,
and there is no language that
God does not understand.

—*Duke Ellington*

## April 30

I watch.
I watch, I wait
and am still,
abiding the cycle that moves
as it will.

The beauties,
the struggles
that most do not see,
the hidden and secret
are open to me.

The new and the full and the dark
of the moon,
the shapes in the shadows,
the brightness of noon
all have their place
in the turning of time...
both coming and going
have reason
and rhyme.

The herbs of the field and the
symbols of land
bring healing and bless
as they come through my hand.

I welcome the fruits,
I welcome new birth,
as old wounds are healed
in the joy
of the earth.

> —*Nancy Rose Meeker,*
> *"The Healer"*

**May 1**

*May Day*

> Whenever evil befalls us, we ought to ask ourselves,
> after the first suffering, how we can turn it into good.
> So shall we take occasion, from one bitter root, to raise
> perhaps many flowers.
>
> —*Leigh Hunt*

**May 2**

> Let us think of Mother Earth, her rich bounty that will
> result from springtime, the golden corn and the seeds
> of harvest, all grown strong from Mother Earth, the
> spring rains, and the energy of Father Sky. It is time to
> consider healing: healing of ourselves, healing of a
> loved one, healing of adversaries for peace among
> nations, and healing of the harms done to Mother
> Earth.
>
> > Oh, Great Spirit,
> > I pray for myself in order that I may be healed.
> > Oh, Great Spirit,
> > I pray for my close friend who is sick and
> >     needs help.

Oh, Great Spirit,
I pray for this world so that all these atomic
    weapons
And other bad things that we point at each
    other
Will someday soon all be destroyed.
I pray that adversaries will communicate
And all of the mistrust will be healed.
Oh, Great Spirit,
I pray for the environment.
I pray for its cleansing
And the renewal of our Mother Earth.

—*Ed McGaa, Eagle Man*

### May 3

Weaver God, we come to you,
or more the truth—you find us,
disconnected and out of sorts.
We are disheartened by our failures,
discouraged by our weakness
    and little that we do seems worthy of your
    grace.
Restore our fortunes. Restore our future.
Weave for us the tapestry
    on which our lives are stretched.

Give us patience with the endless
    back and forth of shuttle, hand and effort.
We look too closely, seeing only strands and knots
and snarled threads of too-much-trying
or none-at-all.
Grant us eyes to see the whole
    of which we are a part.
In the end, we ask for gentleness with ourselves,
acceptance of our less than perfect ways.
We pray that what we do
and what you weave form patterns clear to all,
of mercy in the warp of it
and love throughout.

—Pat Kozak and Janet Schaffran

**May 4**

Friend, you lie quiet,
watching the dawn light color your heart,
dreaming of healing for your hurt body
laying there unanswerable to your will.
You breathe deep and your breath has two sides:
    inside and outside. You are on both, being
    breathed.
The future approaches. You will heal or
you will go back to being God.
Which will you do?

Oh by all that is beautiful—
May it be that you live!
May your body heal happy and whole!
May energy fill and delight you!
May we join the dance your presence gives!
May you live!

And if you die?
Oh dear self, by all that is beautiful,
Know you are Safe! Everything is All Right
Forever and Ever and Ever!
The most wonderful, exquisite, familiar
Truth is what is True, and welcomes you.
It will be very easy.

You lie quiet now, praying.
A great healing is coming
and you want to be ready.
The colors of your heart blend
with the light of the morning.
You are blessed.

—*Elias Amidon*

**May 5**

*Said after Holy Communion:*
This morning my soul is greater than the world since it
possesses You, You whom heaven and earth do not
contain.

—*Saint Margaret of Cortona*

**May 6**

*Enlightenment of the
Buddha is celebrated*

May every creature abound in well-being and peace.
May every living being, weak or strong, the long and
    the small
The short and the medium-sized, the mean and the
    great
May every living being, seen or unseen, those dwelling
    far off,
Those near by, those already born, those waiting to be
    born
May all attain inward peace.

Let no one deceive another
Let no one despise another in any situation
Let no one, from antipathy or hatred,
    wish evil to anyone at all.

Just as a mother, with her own life,
        protects her only son from hurt
So within yourself foster a limitless concern
        for every living creature.
Display a heart of boundless love for all the world
In all its height and depth and broad extent
Love unrestrained, without hate or enmity.
Then as you stand or walk, sit or lie,
        until overcome by drowsiness
Devote your mind entirely to this,
        it is known as living here life divine.

—*The Buddha*

**May 7**

Dear God,
Be my redeemer, my internal teacher, my divine
        physician.
Thank You for Your presence in my life.
I surrender to You all I am, all I think, all I feel, and all
        I have.
I recognize in this moment that Yours is the power to
        heal and make whole.
You who have the power to work miracles, You who
        rule time and space, please take me in Your
        arms and hold me.
Dear Lord, please lift me up and heal me.

Cast out of my mind all thoughts that are not of You.
Cast out of me all harsh and critical nature.
Cast out of me all violence and all anger.
Cast out of me all demons from my past.
For I would be made new.
I wish to walk so close to You that we might be as
    one.
I ask for new life, new mind, new body, new spirit.
Dear God, please come into me and release me from
    this pain.
Amen.

—*Marianne Williamson*


**May 8**

It is the enemy who can truly teach us to practice the
virtues of compassion and tolerance.

—*The Dalai Lama*


**May 9**

Spirit of truth,
you are the reward to the saints,
the comforter of souls,
light in the darkness,
riches to the poor,

treasure to lovers,
food for the hungry,
comfort to the wanderer;
to sum up,
you are the one in whom all treasures are contained.

—*Saint Mary Magdalen dei Pazzi*

**May 10**

Beehive source
Trellised womb
Mother of all beginnings

Hold me
Gather me
Feed me
With the honey-nectar
From the hive.

Nourished
I will sing
The Bee-song
The long-forgotten threnody
Of praise to thee.

—*Anne Baring*

**May 11**

Mother of gods, father of gods, Ancient God,
A mere appendage of the realm, a common man, has
    come.
He comes crying, he comes in sadness, he comes with
    guilt.
Perhaps he has slipped, perhaps he has stumbled,
perhaps he has touched the bird of evil, the spider's
    web, the tuft of thorns:
It wounds his heart, it troubles him.
Master, Lord,
Ever Present, Ever Near,
Take it from him: hear the pain of this common man.

*—Aztec prayer*

**May 12**
*In 1935, Alcoholics Anonymous
is founded by William Wilson
in Akron, Ohio*

God, I offer myself to Thee—to build with me and to
do with me as Thou wilt. Relieve me of the bondage
of self, that I may better do Thy will. Take away my dif-
ficulties, that victory over them may bear witness to
those I would help of Thy Power, Thy Love, and Thy
Way of life. May I do Thy will always!

*—Alcoholics Anonymous
(Page 63)*

**May 13**

Thou art the mysterious Electricity of my body, moving the intricate mechanism of flesh, bones, muscles, and nerves. Thy life force is present in my every breath and heartbeat. O Sole Doer in Man and the Universe! may I realize that all power is divine and flows only from Thee.

> —*Yogananda,*
> *Whispers from Eternity*

**May 14**

O Lord,
>    open my eyes that I may see the needs of
>        others;
>    open my ears that I may hear their cries;
>    open my heart so that they need not be without
>        succor.

>    let me not be afraid to defend the weak because
>            of the anger of the strong, nor afraid to
>    defend the poor because of the anger of the rich.

Show me where love and hope and faith are needed,
>    and use me to bring them to those places.

And so open my eyes and my ears
    that I may this coming day be able to do some
    work of peace for thee.
Amen.

—*Alan Paton*

**May 15**

Do you need Me? I am there.

You cannot see Me, yet I am the light you see by.
You cannot hear Me, yet I speak through your voice.
You cannot feel me, yet I am the power
    at work in your hands.

I am at work, though you do not understand My
    ways.
I am at work, though you do not recognize My
    works.
I am not strange visions. I am not mysteries.
Only in absolute stillness, beyond self,
Can you know Me as I am,
and then but as a feeling and a faith.

Yet I am there. Yet I am here. Yet I answer.

When you need Me, I am there.
Even if you deny Me, I am there.

Even when you feel most alone, I am there.
Even in your fears, I am there.
Even in your pain, I am there.
I am there when you pray and when you do not pray.

Though your faith in Me is unsure,
My faith in you never wavers,
because I know you, because I love you.

Beloved, I am there.

—*James Dillet Freeman*

**May 16**

A prominent Jewish prayer concludes "May He who
made peace in the heavens grant peace to us on earth."
What does it mean to create peace in the heavens?
Ancient man looked up into the sky and he saw the
sun and the rainclouds. And he would say to himself
"How can fire and water, sun and rain co-exist in the
same sky? Either the water would put out the fire, or
the fire would dry up the water." How do they get
along? It must be a miracle. The sun says, "If I dry up
the rainclouds, as I probably could, the world will not
survive without rain." The clouds say, "If we extinguish
the sun, the world will perish in darkness." So the fire
and the water make peace, realizing that if either one

of them achieved a total victory, the world could not endure.

When we pray for God to grant us the sort of peace He ordained in the heavens, this is the miracle we ask for. How can men and women live together happily? They are opposites; their needs are different, their rhythms are different. It takes a miracle for them to bridge those differences and unite the masculine side of God's image with the feminine side.

How can Arabs and Israelis learn to live together? Irish Catholics and Irish Protestants? Black South Africans and white South Africans? It takes a miracle for them to realize that if they won, if they had it all and the other side had nothing, the world could not survive their victory. Only by making room for everyone in the world, even for our enemies, can the world survive.

May God who showed us the miracle of Shalom, of making room for each other and giving up the illusion of victory in the heavens, grant a similar miracle to all of us who inhabit the earth.

—*Rabbi Harold S. Kushner*

**May 17**

What is healing but the removal
of all that stands in the way of knowledge?
And how else can one dispel illusions
except by looking at them directly,
without protecting them?
Be not afraid, therefore,
for what you will be looking at
is the source of fear,
and you are beginning to learn
that fear is not real.

> —*From A Course in Miracles*
> *(Text, page 188)*

114

**May 18**

I have come to terms with the future.
From this day onward I will walk
easy on the earth. Plant trees. Kill
no living things. Live in harmony with
all creatures. I will restore the earth
where I am. Use no more of its resources
than I need. And listen, listen to what
it is telling me.

> —*M.J. Slim Hooey*

## May 19

He giveth power to the faint; and to them that have no
might He increaseth strength.

*—Isaiah 40:29*

## May 20

I am the unopened bud, and I the blossom,
    I am the lifeforce gathering to a crest,
I am the still companion of the silence,
    I am the farflung seeker of the quest.
I am the daughter gathering in wisdom,
    I am the son whose questions never cease,
I am the dawn-light searching out glad justice,
    I am the center where all souls find peace.

*—Caitlin Matthews*

## May 21

O God, my God! I beg of Thee by the ocean of
Thy healing, and by the splendors of the Daystar of
Thy grace, and by Thy Name through which Thou
didst subdue Thy servants, and by the pervasive power
of Thy most exalted Word and the potency of Thy
most august Pen, and by Thy mercy that hath preceded
the creation of all who are in heaven and on earth, to

purge me with the waters of Thy bounty from every
affliction and disorder, and from all weakness and feebleness.

Thou seest, O my Lord, Thy suppliant waiting at
the door of Thy bounty, and him who hath set his
hopes on Thee clinging to the cord of Thy generosity.
Deny him not, I beseech Thee, the things he seeketh
from the ocean of Thy grace and the Daystar of Thy
loving-kindness.

Powerful art Thou to do what pleaseth Thee.
There is none other God save Thee, the Ever-
Forgiving, the Most Generous.

—*Baha'u'llah*


**May 22**

At times I feel the winds of illness
    have made a barren landscape of
    my life.
I can no longer see mountains to be
    climbed in the distance.

But then I look around me and
    I realize that I am soaring
    above the mountains.

They look so small from my new
     perspective.

       *—Judith Garrett Garrison and*
         *Scott Sheperd*


## May 23

Great one, who became Heaven,
Thou didst assume power;
     thou didst stir;
Thou hast filled all places
     with thy beauty.
The whole earth lies beneath thee.
Thou hast taken possession of it.
Thou enclosest the earth
     and all things in thy arms.

        *—H. Frankfort*


## May 24

May all things move and be moved in me
     and know and be known in me
May all creation
     dance for joy within me.

        *—Chinook Psalter*

**May 25**

Become conscious for a single moment that Life and intelligence are purely spiritual,—neither in nor of matter,—and the body will then utter no complaints. If suffering from a belief in sickness, you will find yourself suddenly well. Sorrow is turned into joy when the body is controlled by spiritual Life, Truth, and Love.

> —*Mary Baker Eddy,*
> *Science and Health with*
> *Key to the Scriptures*

**May 26**
*In 604, Saint*
*Augustine dies*

God of life, there are days when the burdens we carry chafe our shoulders and wear us down; when the road seems dreary and endless, the skies gray and threatening; when our lives have no music in them and our hearts are lonely, and our souls have lost their courage. Flood the path with light, we beseech you; turn our eyes to where the skies are full of promise.

> —*Saint Augustine*

## May 27

I have no other helper than you,
no other father,
no other redeemer,
no other support.
I pray to you.
Only you can help me.
My present misery
is too great.
Despair grips me,
and I am at my wits' end.
I am sunk in the depths,
and I cannot pull myself up
or out.
If it is your will,
help me out of this misery.
Let me know
that you are stronger
than all misery and all enemies.
O Lord, if I come through this,
please let the experience
contribute to my and my brothers' blessing.
You will not forsake me;
this I know.
Amen.

—*Ghana*

119

## May 28

In the name of Raven. In the name of Wolf. In the name of Whale. In the name of Snake. Who have taught us. Who have guided us. Who have sustained us. Who have healed us.

Please heal the animals.

In the name of Raven. In the name of Wolf. In the name of Whale. In the name of Snake. Whom we have slaughtered. Whom we have feared. Whom we have caged. Whom we have persecuted. Whom we have slandered. Whom we have cursed. Whom we have tortured.

Please protect the animals.

In the name of Raven. In the name of Wolf. In the name of Whale. In the name of Snake. Whose habitat we have stolen. Whose territory we have plundered. Whose feeding grounds we have paved and netted. Whose domain we have poisoned. Whose food we have appropriated. Whose young we have killed. Whose lives and ways of life we have threatened.

Please restore the animals.

In the name of Raven. In the name of Wolf. In the name of Whale. In the name of Snake.

Forgive us. Have mercy. May the animals return.
Not as a resurrection but as living beings. On earth.
On this earth that is also theirs.
Oh Great Spirit. Please heal the animals. Please protect
the animals. Please restore the animals.
So our lives may also be healed. So our souls may be
protected. So our spirits may be restored.
Oh Spirit of Raven. Oh Spirit of Wolf. Oh Spirit of
Whale. Oh Spirit of Snake.

Teach us, again, how to live.

—*Deena Metzger*


**May 29**

Why restless, why cast down, my soul?
Hope still, and thou shalt sing
The praise of Him who is thy God
Thy health's eternal spring.

—*Nahum Tate*

**May 30**

*In 1869, Memorial Day,*
*or Decoration Day,*
*is first observed in the*
*United States*

Dear God,
with you everything is possible.
Let the cup of war,
killing, and destruction,
the cup of bloodshed,
human anguish and desolation,
the cup of torture,
breakage in human relationships and abandonment...
Dear God,
let this cup pass us by.
We are afraid.
We are trembling in the depths of our being.
We feel the sweat and tears
of thousands of people all over the world,
people who are afraid—
afraid to fight,
afraid to kill,
afraid of being killed,
afraid of an uncertain future.

*—Henri J.M. Nouwen*

**May 31**

> Beloved Lord, Almighty God!
> Through the rays of the sun,
> Through the waves of the air,
> Through the All-pervading Life in space,
> Purify and revivify me, and, I pray.
> Heal my body, heart, and soul.
>> Amen.
>
> —*Hazrat Inayat Khan*

**June 1**
*U.S. author and activist*
*Helen Keller dies in 1968*

> I thank God for my handicaps, for, through them, I
> have found myself, my work, and my God.
>
> —*Helen Keller*

**June 2**

> Peace between neighbors,
> Peace between kindred,
> Peace between lovers,
> In the love of the King of life.

Peace between person and person,
Peace between wife and husband,
Peace between women and children,
The peace of Christ above all peace.

Bless, O Christ, my face,
Let my face bless everything;
Bless, O Christ, mine eye,
Let mine eye bless all it sees.

124                           —*Gaelic, date unknown*

### June 3

In safety and in Bliss
May all creatures be of a blissful heart
Whatever breathing beings there may be
Frail or firm...long or big...short or small
Seen or unseen, dwelling far or near
Existing or yet seeking to exist
May all creatures be of a blissful heart.

—*Sutta Nipata*

### June 4

As a mother shall she meet him...
With the Bread of Understanding
    shall she feed him,

And give him the Water of Wisdom
    to drink.

                *—Wisdom of Jesus Ben Sirach 15:2-3*

## June 5
*World*
*Environment*
*Day*

May the Holy Spirit guide us as we seek to heal and
to nurture the earth and all of its creatures, to live in
the midst of creation, and to love one another as
brothers and sisters with all life.

                *—U.N. Environmental Sabbath*

## June 6

We are aware that all generations of our ancestors
and all future generations are present in us.

We are aware of the expectations that our
ancestors, our children, and their children have of us.

We are aware that our joy, peace, freedom, and
harmony are the joy, peace, freedom, and harmony
of our ancestors, our children, and their children.

We are aware that understanding is the very
foundation of love.

We are aware that blaming and arguing never help
us and only create a wider gap between us, that
only understanding, trust, and love can help us
change and grow.

—*Thich Nhat Hanh*

126

## June 7

The reality that is present to us and in us:
call it Being... Silence.
And the simple fact that by being attentive,
by learning to listen
(or recovering the natural capacity to listen)
we can find ourself engulfed in such happiness
that it cannot be explained:
the happiness of being at one with everything
in that hidden ground of Love
for which there can be no explanations....
May we all grow in grace and peace,
and not neglect the silence that is printed
in the centre of our being.
It will not fail us.

—*Thomas Merton*

## June 8

*Mohammed, prophet
and founder of Islam,
dies in 632*

> O God, give me, I pray Thee,
> light on my right hand
> and light on my left hand
> and light above me
> and light beneath me,
> O Lord, increase light within me
> and give me light
> and illuminate me.

> *—Ascribed to Mohammad*

## June 9

> When I awake in the morning,
> It is either the very next day
> after many, many days,
> Or it is the very first day.
> When it is the very next day
> after many, many days,
> I know the time has come
> For me to walk through the door,
> To take a look at that dark part of me
> that is calling.
> And to touch that place of willingness

to look again.
I know the time has come
For me to walk through the door
To take a look at this critic within,
Who only wants me to listen
To what needs to be heard,
So I then can heal
and bring that part of me
back to me.

When I awake in the morning,
It is either the very next day
after many, many days
Or it is the very first day.
Today, it is the very first day
Of what exists now.

> —*Twainhart Hill,*
> *"An Ode to My Father*
> *Healing the Critic"*

## June 10

If I were alone in a desert
    and feeling afraid,
I would want a child to be with me.
For then my fear would disappear
    and I would be made strong.
This is what life in itself can do

because it is so noble, so full of pleasure
        and so powerful.
But if I could not have a child with me
I would like to have at least a living animal
at my side to comfort me.

Therefore,
let those who bring about wonderful things
in their big, dark books
take an animal
to help them.
The life within the animal
will give them strength in turn.
        For equality
gives strength, in all things
and at all times.

—*Meister Eckhart*

## June 11

*U.S. author William*
*Styron is born in 1925*

> For those who have dwelt in depression's dark wood,
> and known its inexplicable agony, their return from the
> abyss is not unlike the ascent of the poet, trudging
> upward and upward out of hell's black depths and at
> last emerging into what he saw as "the shining world."

There, whoever has been restored to health has almost always been restored to the capacity for serenity and joy, and this may be indemnity enough for having endured the despair beyond despair.

> *E quindi uscimmo a riveder le stelle.*
> *And so we came forth, and once again beheld*
> *the stars.*

> —*William Styron*

## June 12

> Some nights, stay up till dawn,
> as the moon sometimes does for the sun.
> Be a full bucket pulled up the dark way
> of a well, then lifted out into light.
>
> Something opens our wings. Something
> makes boredom and hurt disappear.
> Someone fills the cup in front of us.
> We taste only sacredness.

> —*Rumi*
> *Translated by John Moyne*
> *and Coleman Barks*

## June 13

*Saint Anthony of Padua*
*dies in 1231*

> Lord Jesus, bind us to you and to our neighbor with
>     love.
> May our hearts not be turned away from you.
> May our souls not be deceived nor our talents or
>     minds enticed by allurements of error, so that
>     we may never distance ourselves from your love.
> Thus may we love our neighbor as ourselves with
>     strength, wisdom and gentleness. With your
>     help, you who are blessed throughout all ages.
>
> —*Saint Anthony of Padua*

## June 14

*Flag Day (U.S.)*

> Your face is the only fatherland for me.
>
> —*Saint Therese of Lisieux*

## June 15

God, make me brave for life: oh, braver than this.
Let me straighten after pain, as a tree straightens after
      the rain,
Shining and lovely again.
God, make me brave for life; much braver than this.
As the blown grass lifts, let me rise
From sorrow with quiet eyes,
Knowing Thy way is wise.
God, make me brave, life brings
Such blinding things.
Help me to keep my sight;
Help me to see aright
That out of dark comes light.

*—Author unknown*

## June 16

Dear God, we give thanks for places of simplicity and
peace. Let us find such a place within ourselves. We
give thanks for places of refuge and beauty. Let us find
such a place within ourselves. We give thanks for places
of nature's truth and freedom, of joy, inspiration and
renewal, places where all creatures may find acceptance
and belonging. Let us search for these places: in the
world, in ourselves and in others. Let us restore them.

Let us strengthen and protect them and let us create them.

May we mend this outer world according to the truth of our inner life and may our souls be shaped and nourished by nature's eternal wisdom. Amen.

—*Leunig*

## June 17

*English founder of Methodism John Wesley is born in 1703*

Do all the good you can,
By all the means you can,
In all the ways you can,
In all the places you can,
To all the people you can.
As long as ever you can.

—*John Wesley*

## June 18

My help is in the mountain
Where I take myself to heal
The earthly wounds

That people give to me.
I find a rock with sun on it
And a stream where the water runs gentle
And the trees which one by one give me company.
So must I stay for a long time
Until I have grown from the rock
And the stream is running through me
And I cannot tell myself from one tall tree.
Then I know that nothing touches me

Nor makes me run away.
My help is in the mountain
That I take away with me.

Earth cure me. Earth receive my woe. Rock strengthen
me. Rock receive my weakness. Rain wash my sadness
away. Rain receive my doubt. Sun make sweet my
song. Sun receive the anger from my heart.

—*Nancy Wood*


**June 19**

They say a child is born
a blank shape to be molded,
a tabula rasa to be written upon.
But children come
like a plant with a rhizome—
its food source,

the genetic coding for what flower it will become,
how often it will bear fruit,
what its artistry is;
all of that born into it with the seed.
The role of the gardener, then,
is simply to discern the manner of plant
or child trying to emerge.
The role of the gardener,
or parent then,
is simply to ask,
"How do I help it grow
into what it is in its roots?"

—Dawna Markova

## June 20

Earth, ourselves,
breathe and awaken,
leaves are stirring,
all things moving,
new day coming,
life renewing.

—Pawnee prayer

SUMMER

**June 21**

*Summer Solstice*

> May your life be like a
>     wildflower,
> growing freely in the
>     beauty
> and joy of each day.

> —*Native American proverb*

138

**June 22**

> We are one, after all, you and I;
> together we suffer,
> together exist,
> and forever will recreate each other.

> —*Pierre Teilhard de Chardin*

## June 23

From nothingness, from the play of molecules
    in evolution,
passed through countless generations, tokens of
vitality and form, my seed atoms came from you.
Carried on a wave of chance, coincidence
    and hidden necessity,
my portion of cosmic dust passed through you.
I am awed by the miracle at each step
    that leads to my being. Yet here I am!
    And so, you are.
I am the messenger of my father and mother,
    a conduit for your future, and through this
    you live in me.
Not just the stuff of your genes, but the stuff
    of your dreams, too.
For as I feel the years imprint their inevitable marks
    on my skin,
I look more honestly and clearly into my soul
    and see you.
I feel your fears and sorrows in my chest, caught in
    the intake of my breath, thumping in my heart;
I feel your cherished joys pumping through my veins
when I hear a favorite song,
    after I've run along my Skyline,
when I look out on the waves, or face the sun
    and feel it warm my smile.

If I'm quiet and still enough, I can feel you
        living through me.
I recognize your spirit stirring memories,
        emotions and desires.
Sometimes I look out on my world as if my eyes
are windows to our common soul.
I share this with you in gratitude and love.
        Always.

> —Christian de Quincey,
> "From You, Through Me, To You:
> To My Parents, Donnie and Rita"

## June 24
*Saint John of the Cross
is born in 1542*

> And I saw the river
> over which every soul must pass
> to reach the kingdom of heaven
> and the name of that river was suffering:—
> and I saw the boat
> which carries souls across the river
> and the name of that boat was
> love.

> —Saint John of the Cross

**June 25**

From the depths of holy silence, I give thanks for the joy and energy of life. May all beings enjoy the vitality of their existence.

I remember all who suffer great pain and long-term illness, especially [names]. May the Healer of Hurts breathe balm and restoration into all wounded lives.

May all negative, angry and harmful attitutes, especially my . . . . . . . . that I harbor within me be transformed into new and available life.

The dance of a Summer day calls my steps: may I respond to the rhythm and melody of its music.

—*Caitlin Matthews*

**June 26**
*In 1945, the U.N. Charter
is signed by 50 nations in
San Francisco*

May there be peace in the higher regions; may there be peace in the firmament; may there be peace on earth. May the waters flow peacefully; may the herbs and plants grow peacefully; may all the divine powers bring unto us peace. The supreme Lord is peace. May we all

be in peace, peace, and only peace; and may that peace
come unto each of us.

Shanti (peace)—Shanti—Shanti!

—*The Vedas*
*Translated by*
*Raimundo Panniker*

## June 27

May the
longtime
sun shine upon you,
all love surround you,
and the sweet light within you
guide your way on.

—*Traditional blessing*

## June 28

A small wave for your form
A small wave for your voice
A small wave for your speech
A small wave for your means
A small wave for your generosity
A small wave for your appetite

A small wave for your wealth
   A small wave for your life
      A small wave for your health.
Nine waves of grace upon you.
Waves of the Giver of Health.

—*Mhairi nic Neill*

## June 29

Do you imagine the universe is agitated?
Go into the desert at night and look out at the stars.
This practice should answer the question.

The superior person settles her mind as the universe
   settles the stars in the sky.
By connecting her mind with the subtle origin, she
   calms it.
Once calmed, it naturally expands, and ultimately her
   mind becomes as vast and immeasurable as the
   night sky.

—*Lao-Tzu*
*Translated by Brian Walker*

**June 30**

Plants and Animal in the Garden,
We welcome you—we invite you in—we ask your
  forgiveness and your understanding. Listen as we
  invoke your names, as we also listen for you:
Little sparrows, quail, robins and house finches who
  have died in our strawberry nets;
Young Cooper's Hawk who flew into our sweet pea
  trellis and broke your neck;
Numerous orange-bellied newts who died by our
  shears, in our irrigation pipes, by our cars, and
  by our feet;
Slugs and snails whom we have pursued for years,
  feeding you to the ducks, crushing you,
  trapping you, picking you off and tossing you
  over our fences;
Gophers and moles, trapped and scorned by us, and
  also watched with love, admiration, and awe
  for your one-mindedness;
Sowbugs, spitbugs, earwigs, flea beetles, woolly
  aphids, rose-suckers, cutworms, millipedes
  and other insects whom we have lured and
  stopped;
Snakes and moths who have been caught in our water
  system and killed by our mowers;
Families of mice who have died in irrigation pipes, by
  electricity in our pump box, and by predators
  while nesting in our greenhouses;

Manure worms and earthworms, severed by spades,
and numerous microscopic lifeforms in our
compost system who have been burned by
sunlight;

Feral cats and raccoons whom we've steadily chased
from the garden;

Rats whom we poisoned and trapped and drowned.
Deer, chased at dawn and at midnight, routed by
dogs, by farmers, by fences and numerous
barriers;

Plants: colored lettuces, young broccoli, ripe
strawberries and sweet apples, all of you who
have lured the animals to your sides, and all
plants we have shunned: poison hemlock,
pigweed, bindweed, stinging nettle, bull
thistle;

We call up plants we have removed by dividing you
and separating you, and deciding you no
longer grow well here;

We invoke you and thank you and continue to learn
from you. We dedicate this ceremony to you. We
will continue to practice with you and for you.

—*Wendy Johnson, Green Gulch Farm*

## July 1

> Be tough in the way a blade of grass is: rooted, willing to lean, and at peace with what is around it.

> —*Natalie Goldberg*

## July 2

*In 1937, U.S. aviator*
*Amelia Earhart disappears*
*over the Pacific*

> Courage is the price that life exacts for granting peace.
> The soul that knows it not, knows no release
> From little things;
> Knows not the livid loneliness of fear,
> Nor mountain heights where bitter joy can hear
> The sound of wings.

> —*Amelia Earhart*

## July 3

> Although my spirit may wander the four corners of
> the earth,
> Let it come back to me again so that I may live and
> journey here.

Although my spirit may go far away over the sea,
Let it come back to me again so that I may live and
    journey here.

Although my spirit may go far away to the flashing
    beams of light,
Let it come back to me again so that I may live and
    journey here.

Although my spirit may go far away to visit the sun
    and the dawn,
Let it come back to me again so that I may live and
    journey here.

Although my spirit may wander over the lofty
    mountains,
Let it come back to me again so that I may live and
    journey here.

Although my spirit may go far away into all forms
    that live and move,
Let it come back to me again so that I may live and
    journey here.

Although my spirit may go far away to distant
    realms,
Let it come back to me again so that I may live and
    journey here.

Although my spirit may go far away to all that is and
    is to be,

Let it come back to me again so that I may live and
journey here.

Although my spirit may wander in the valley of
death,
Let it come back to me again so that I may live and
journey here.

*—Hymn from the ancient Rig-Veda*

## July 4

*Independence Day
(United States)*

*We ask you to join with us daily at noon (12 p.m. EST),
wherever you are, for three minutes of prayer and meditation
for the future of the United States, with the following prayer:*

May we as a nation be guided by the Divine to redis
cover the sacred flame of our national heritage,
which so many have given their lives to safeguard;

Let the wounds of separation and division be healed by
opening our hearts to listen to the truth on all
sides, allowing us to find a higher truth that
includes us all;

May we learn to honor and enjoy our diversity and
differences as a people, even as we more deeply
touch our fundamental unity;

May we, as a people, undergo a transformation that will
draw forth individuals to lead our nation who
embody courage, compassion, and a higher vision;

May our leaders inspire us, and we so inspire each
other with our potential as individuals and as a
nation, that a new spirit of forgiveness, caring, and
honesty be born in our nation;

May we, as a united people, move with clear, directed
purpose to take our place within the community 149
of nations to help build a better future for all
humankind;

May we as a nation rededicate ourselves to truly living
as one nation, under God, indivisible, with liberty
and justice for all;

And may God's Will be done for the United States, as
we, the people, align with that Will.

—*Corinne McLaughlin and*
*Gordon Davidson*

### July 5

—a phantom, dew, a bubble,
A dream, a flash of lightning, and a cloud;
Thus we should look upon all that was made.

—*The Buddha*

## July 6

All shall be well
and all shall be well
and all manner of thing shall be well.

—*Blessed Julian of Norwich*

## July 7

*In 1535, Saint
Thomas More is
beheaded for refusing
to acknowledge Henry VIII
as the supreme authority
of the Church*

Almighty God, have mercy on [name]
and on all that bear me evil will and would do me
    harm,
and on their faults and mine together.
By such easy, tender, merciful means as your own
    infinite wisdom can best devise;
vouchsafe to amend and redress and make us saved
    souls in heaven together.
Where we may ever live and love together with you
    and your blessed saints.

—*Saint Thomas More
"On Behalf of an Enemy"*

## July 8

Deep in the sunburst heart of the covered bazaar, the last of the weary shopkeepers are closing their doors for the Ramadan holiday. The dusty maze of streets is so quiet I can hear the shuffle of my own sandals. Near the Djama el Fna Plaza, I find four blind drummakers leaning against a wooden cart. They are shadow-striped by the afternoon light coming in through the slatted roof of the market. They are playing wooden flutes, a slender-necked rebeck, jangly tambourines, and goat-skin drums of many sizes. They are singing folk songs as old as the desert. Their long windstorm-bent fingers clutch moist wild figs and glasses of tea with floating mint sprigs. Their self-assured smiles are strong enough to prop up the crumbling walls of the *medina*. The oldest among them is a Bedouin nomad with a dusty beard and a rhythm on his drum that sounds like an approaching sandstorm. His head sways back and forth in and out of the slanting light, as if listening to the bells of a distant camel caravan. Hearing my tentative approach, he gestures for me to come out of the shadows. I lean down to hear him. Softly, he says, *With hands, is Marrakesh way. For feeling. No feeling with sticks. Just with hands comes feeling, for drumming.*

I watch his sun-burnished hands dancing over the taut drumskin as if they're circling God, hear his voice push the prayer high into the impossibly blue skies above the towering red walls of the city of ancient days. *And you, kind sir,* he asks as he pours the steaming tea for me in a long graceful arc. *How do you feel, with your hands?* He drops three sugarcubes into the hot tea glass. *What is your way through the world, for feeling?*

I watch the sugar crystals dissolve slowly, and taste the answer as my hands absorb the heat of the steaming glass, and a rumble begins in the ground below me, as if words were arriving like a prayer from a very great distance, and knocking on the door of my heart.

—*Phil Cousineau,*
*"The Marrakesh Way"*

### July 9

Offer only lovely things on my altars—
the bread of life, and jewels, and feathers, and flowers.
Let the streams of life flow in peace.
Turn from violence.
Learn to think for a long time how to change this
        world,
how to make it better to live in.
All the people in the world ought to talk about it
and speak well of it always.

Then it will last forever,
and the flowers will bloom forever,
and I will come to you again.

—*Quetzalcoatl*

## July 10

*"I think I know you,"*

she said, reaching toward her son, *interrumpiendo el
sueno de una danza con la sida que solo queria disolverle en
su luz,* interrupting a dark dance of a night time
knowing, with this disease called AIDS that had already
begun to dissolve him into its light.

*"I think I know you,"*

she repeated, arousing him from his dreams. *"Hijo
de Picuris y nuevomejico,* son of those who paint, son of
the *arroyos,* son of the *mesas,* and son of the *Sangre de
Cristo* mountains," she said, caressing his hands with her
words.

*"I know you. Yes, I know you,"*

she cooed, soothing him with her knowledge.
*"Recuerdate,* remember," she whispered, *"de la tierra
sagrada,* of sacred land, *y la agua bendita* and the blessed
water." "Remember the strength of your people, *el*

*poder de tu pueblo,"* she offered carefully wrapping his
fingers with memory and story.

Like Tonantzin, read "Virgen de Guadalupe," who left
the Indian Juan Diego the power to heal the *herida
abierta,* the open wound, through painted image

artist, you need only to unfold your hands:
                                                  parting prayer,
and at their feet will fall the image: *La Madre Tierra*—

                        not the roses of *Tonantzin,* but
                        s u n   f l o w e r s,

like you, lovers of light, lovers of movement,
and like you blessed in daily   r e v o l u t i o n s

### I. La Vida, Life

Though marked still with a brother's blood, this Cain is
no longer cursed. Once exiled from the land by towers
rising to the sky,.
                        silencing his tongue,

            Now blessed by the hand of a Tewa Pueblo
            Mother—Ia'tik: *"bringing to life,"* new seeds,

            "Here," she says, "is the root of your new
            tongue." and your new name is:      *"Turning
            Around"*

Tiller of soil, your name is ripe with the summer *maiz*, *frijoles* and *chile*. *La Tierra, que sabe que la quieres, abrazandote, se deja celebrar tu nombre* The earth knows that you love it; embracing you, it celebrates your name,

birthing by your hand,
                    *girasol* and sunflower
            Turning Around, Turning Around

### II. La Muerta, Death

*Jardinero,* today darkness arrives early, unfolding memory from shadows, filling your mouth with the dust of too many losses: deaths still unspoken.

These are the unbroken silences that find refuge in our throats—choking.

                    Yet, born at these cross-roads, yours
                    is a calling of lovers lost and of the
                    cyclic, song of our fugitive faith:

            Turning Around, Turning Around

Alone in the garden, waiting, while your army of sunflowers bow in sleep, unmoved by the shadow of *Dona Sebastiana's* death dance, you lie awake

And though she chased your *So!* away, *lentamente besandote y mordiendote,* like a

jealous lover, pulling yours and the faces of
your army into her own warm and gentle light

*Madre Luna's* kisses will not you tonight betray

### III. *Levantando Caras, Resurrection*

Here, a brush in brown hands, touches upon an incom-
plete, yet storied past. Once dancer, then gardener, now
painter,
>> each drawing still upon this light,

> dancing, the *girasol,* turns on her god as he sets,
> that same look, which she turned when he rose

The rebelliousness of tradition, drawing each into old
*curanderismo*—
>> images as prayer, offering, and
>> ceremony.

like paintings along the

stone walls of the
*Rio Grande,* the
images within the
sacred wall of a
*kiva* and *la iglesia,*
and to the mysteries
and medicine of a
sand painting,
colors still
unbroken.

156

*bajando el ser indo-hispano por este puente*
*—dedos desnudos, rebelando y manchandose de*
*esta tinta. Burlando la Muerte que viene a gotas,*
*y solo curando estas heridas de deseo de pintar,*

Your name and your *remedio* is, like a Sunflower,

Turning Around,   Turning Around,   Turning Around.

> —*Estevan Rael Y Galvez,*
> *"Turning Around"*

## July 11

May God the Father who made us bless us
May God the Son send his healing among us
May God the Holy Spirit move within us and give us
eyes to see with, ears to hear with and hands
that your work might be done.
May we walk and preach the word of God to all.
May the angel of peace watch over us and lead us at
    last
by God's grace to the Kingdom.

> —*Saint Dominic*

**July 12**

Father, thank you for your revelation
    about death
    and illness
    and sorrow.

Thank you for speaking so plainly to us,
    for calling us all friends
    and hovering over us;
    for extending your arms out to us.

We cannot stand on our own;
    we fall into death without you.
    We fall from faith, left to our own.
    We are really friendless without you.

Your extended arms fill us with joy,
    expressing love,
    love caring and carrying,
    asking and receiving our trust.

You have our trust, Father,
    and our faith,
    with our bodies
    and all that we are and possess.

We fear nothing when with you,
    safe to stretch out and help others,
    those troubled in faith,
    those troubled in body.

158

Father, help us to do with our bodies what
    we proclaim,
    that our faith be known to you
    and to others,
    and be effective in all the world.

*—Masai, Tanzania*

## July 13

Spirit of love
That flows against our flesh
Sets it trembling
Moves across it as across grass
Erasing every boundary that we
accept
And swings the doors of our lives
wide—
This is a prayer I sing:
Save our perishing earth!

Spirit that cracks our
singles selves—
Eyes fall down eyes,
Hearts escape through the bars
    of
our ribs
To dart into other bodies—

Save this earth!
The earth is perishing.
This is a prayer I sing.

Spirit that hears each one of us,
Hears all that is—
Listens, listens, hears us out—
Inspire us now!
Our own pulse beats in every
stranger's throat,
And also there within the flowered
ground beneath
        our feet,
And—teach us to listen!—
We can hear it in water, in wood,
and even in stone.
We are earth of this earth, and we
are bone of its bone.
This is a prayer I sing, for we have
forgotten this
        and so
The earth is perishing.

—*Barbara Deming*

**July 14**

O God, I thank thee
for all the creatures thou hast made,
so perfect in their kind—
great animals like the elephant and the rhinoceros,
humorous animals like the camel and the monkey,
friendly ones like the dog and the cat,
working ones like the horse and the ox,
timid ones like the squirrel and the rabbit,
majestic ones like the lion and the tiger,
for birds with their songs.
O Lord give us such love for thy creation,
that love may cast out fear,
and all thy creatures see in man
their priest and friend,
through Jesus Christ our Lord.

—*George Appleton*

**July 15**

I am the boundless ocean.

This way and that,
The wind, blowing where it will,
Drives the ship of the world.

But I am not shaken.

I am the unbounded deep
In whom the waves of all the worlds
Naturally rise and fall.

But I do not rise or fall.

I am the infinite deep
In whom all the worlds
Appear to rise.

Beyond all form,
Forever still.

Even so am I.

*—Ashtavakra Gita,*
*unknown Hindu master*

**July 16**
*Mary Baker Eddy,*
*founder of the Christian*
*Science Church, is born*
*in 1821*

Here let me give what I understand to be the spiritual
sense of the Lord's Prayer:

Our Father which art in heaven,
*Our Father-Mother God, all harmonious,*

Hallowed be Thy name.

> *Adorable One.*

Thy kingdom come.

> *Thy kingdom is come; Thou art ever-present.*

Thy will be done in earth, as it is in heaven.

> *Enable us to know,—as in heaven, so on earth,—*
> *God is omnipotent, supreme.*

Give us this day our daily bread;

> *Give us grace for to-day; feed the famished*
> *affections;*

And forgive us our debts, as we forgive our debtors.

> *And Love is reflected in love;*

And lead us not into temptation, but deliver us from evil;

> *And God leadeth us not into temptation, but*
> *delivereth us from sin, disease, and death.*

For Thine is the kingdom, and the power, and the glory, forever.

> *For God is infinite, all-power, all Life, Truth, Love, over*
> *all, and All.*

> —*Mary Baker Eddy,*
> *Science and Health with Key*
> *to the Scriptures*

## July 17

It may help someone to point out
where he is heading,
but the point is lost
unles he is also helped
to change his direction.
The unhealed healer cannot do this for him,
since he cannot do it for himself.
The only meaningful contribution
the healer can make
is to present an example
of one whose direction
has been changed for him,
and who no longer believes
in nightmares of any kind.

> —*From A Course in Miracles*
> *(Text, page 160)*

## July 18
*English novelist*
*Jane Austen*
*dies in 1817*

Incline us O God!
to think humbly of ourselves,
to be saved only in the examination of our own conduct,

to consider our fellow-creatures with kindness,
and to judge of all they say and do with the charity
which we would desire from them ourselves.

—*Jane Austen*

## July 19

Earth teach me stillness
    as the grasses are stilled with light.
Earth teach me suffering
    as old stones suffer with memory.
Earth teach me humility
    as blossoms are humble with beginning.
Earth teach me caring
    as the mother who secures her young.
Earth teach me courage
    as the tree which stands all alone.
Earth teach me limitation
    as the ant which crawls on the ground.
Earth teach me freedom
    as the eagle which soars in the sky.
Earth teach me resignation
    as the leaves which die in the fall.
Earth teach me regeneration
    as the seed which rises in the spring.
Earth teach me to forget myself
    as melted snow forgets its life.

Earth teach me to remember kindness
as dry fields weep with rain.

—*The Ute of North America*

**July 20**

*Anniversary of humankind's
first landing on the moon
in 1969*

Glorious the moon...
Therefore our thanks
Dark clouds
Come to rest our necks

—*Basho*

**July 21**

We invoke your blessing on all the men and women
who have toiled to build and warm our homes, to
fashion our clothing, and to wrest from sea and land
the food that nourishes us and our children.

We pray you that they may have health and joy,
and hope and love, even as we desire for our loved
ones.

Grant us wisdom to deal justly with every man
and woman whom we face in the business of life.

May we not unknowingly inflict suffering
through selfish indifference or the willful ignorance of
a callous heart...

—*Walter Rauschenbusch*

## July 22

Let there be everywhere our voices, our eyes, our
thoughts, our love, our actions,
breathing hope and victory.

—*Sonia Sanchez*

## July 23

What can I do when I feel the world's harsh breath
    and know
That if I stay too long in its path
My path shall be burned up also.
I must go back to the land again
And find the eagle at home with the rock.
I must climb to the mountaintop
And find the spot where the river begins.
I must lie quietly beside the earth
And find the warmth of its heart.
I must turn my vision to the sky
And find the purpose of clouds.

Then trouble seems far away
And the breath which consumes all beauty
Has passed right over me.

—*Nancy Wood*

## July 24

Ask, and it will be given to you; seek, and you will find; knock, and the door will be opened to you. For everyone who asks, receives; and he who seeks, finds; and to him who knocks, the door will be opened.

—*Matthew 7:7-8*

## July 25

God be in my head and in my understanding
God be in my eyes and in my looking
God be in my mouth and in my speaking
God be in my tongue and in my tasting
God be in my lips and in my greeting

God be in my nose and in my smelling/inhaling
God be in my ears and in my hearing
God be in my neck and in my humbling
God be in my shoulders and in my bearing
God be in my back and in my standing

God be in my arms and in my reaching/receiving
God be in my hands and in my working
God be in my legs and in my walking
God be in my feet and in my grounding
God be in my joints and in my relating

God be in my guts and in my feeling
God be in my bowels and in my forgiving
God be in my loins and in my swiving
God be in my lungs and in my breathing
God be in my heart and in my loving

God be in my skin and in my touching
God be in my flesh and in my paining/pining
God be in my blood and in my living
God be in my bones and in my dying
God be at my end and at my reviving

> —*Extended from the
> traditional prayer by
> Reverend Jim Cotter*

## July 26

As for the passions and studies of the mind; avoid envy;
anxious fears; anger fretting inwards; joys and exhilara-
tions in excess; sadness not communicated. Entertain
hopes; mirth rather than joy; variety of delights, rather
than surfeit of them; wonder and admiration, and

therefore novelties; studies that fill the mind with
splendid and illustrious objects, as histories, fables, and
contemplations of nature.

—*Francis Bacon*

## July 27

Father of all Creation,
You have gifted us with grace
And a noble perfection.
But we have lost sight of our original state
And find ourselves trapped in a dark world of
Our own making.

Come, and be soothing balm for our weary bodies.
Enlighten the murkiness of our minds.
Heal the woundedness of our hearts.
Restore the blessedness of our souls.
Show us the way into the splendid Light.
Illuminate our paths to
Your shining Glory.

—*Richard R. Bunbury*

## July 28

Creator, I speak to YOU from within my Soul and
within my Body, asking that I may be an instrument of

peace. May others join together to honor Earth Mother, to keep the skies clean and clear, that She may be nourished. May all creatures of the Earth benefit from the water which is Her blood, flowing through her arteries and veins on the surface and within Her body. May pure water nourish the vegetation, from the tiniest invisible form to the most mighty of all trees on Earth. May all creatures within the soil, within the water, on the land, in the trees and in the air prosper. May They and We be of service to Her good health for future generations.

Creator, shine through us as we join in Your Spirit. Help us all remember, one by one, that we are created of the Earth, and powered by Your Spirit. In this remembering, our separation will end and we will unite in Spirit to restore and care for our Earth Mother, all Her life forms and ourselves.

—*H. Silver Fox Metté*

**July 29**

May my body
Be a prayerstick
For the world.

—*Joan Halifax*

## July 30

There is a force within that gives you life—
    Seek that.
In your body there lies a priceless jewel—
    Seek that.
Oh, wandering Sufi.
    if you are in search of the greatest treasure,
    don't look outside,
Look within, and seek That.

          —*Rumi*
          *Translated by Jonathan Star*

## July 31

Oh, you of wounded spirits,
I offer you a place of rest;
Walk among my mountains,
And climb to Eagle's nest.
Come swim my oceans,
Or feel my desert's fire.
Sit beside running waters
To reclaim your heart's desire.
Seek my silent forests,
Or walk my open plains,
Travel the deepest jungles
'Til you hear my love's refrain.
I am always waiting

172

To allow each child to heal,
To cradle the wounded spirits,
And teach them how to feel.
I am the Earth Mother,
Who loves without regret,
Tending all my children,
Who through tears
     have paid all debts.

             *—Jamie Sams*

## August 1
*U.S. poet Theodore*
*Roethke dies in 1963*

I thirst by day. I watch by night.
I receive! I have been received!
I hear the flowers drinking in their light,
I have taken counsel of the crab and the sea-urchin,
I recall the falling of small waters,
The stream slipping beneath the mossy logs,
Winding down to the stretch of irregular sand,
The great logs piled like matchsticks.

I am most immoderately married:
The Lord God has taken my heaviness away:
I have merged, like the bird, with the bright air,
And my thought flies to the place by the bo-tree.

Being, not doing, is my first job.

          *—Theodore Roethke*

**August 2**

> We call upon the earth, our planet home, with its
> > beautiful depths and soaring heights, its vitality
> > and abundance of life, and together we ask that it:

Teach us, and show us the way.

> We call upon the mountains, the Cascades and the
> > Olympics, the high green valleys and meadows
> > filled with wild flowers, the snows that never
> > melt, the summits of intense silence, and we ask
> > that they:

Teach us, and show us the way.

> We call upon the waters that rim the earth, horizon to
> > horizon, that flow in our rivers and streams, that
> > fall upon our gardens and fields, and we ask that
> > they:

Teach us, and show us the way.

> We call upon the land which grows our food, the nur-
> > turing soil, the fertile fields, the abundant gardens
> > and orchards, and we ask that they:

Teach us, and show us the way.

> We call upon the forests, the great trees reaching
> > strongly to the sky with earth in their roots and

the heavens in their branches, the fir and the pine
and the cedar, and we ask them to:

Teach us, and show us the way.

We call upon the creatures of the fields and forests and
the seas, our brothers and sisters the wolves and
deer, the eagle and dove, the great whales and the
dolphin, the beautiful Orca and salmon who share
our Northwest home, and we ask them to:

Teach us, and show us the way.

We call upon all those who have lived on this earth,
our ancestors and our friends, who dreamed the
best for future generations, and upon whose lives
our lives are built, and with thanksgiving, we call
upon them to:

Teach us, and show us the way.

And lastly, we call upon all that we hold most sacred,
the presence and power of the Great Spirit of love
and truth which flows through all the
universe . . . to be with us to:

Teach us, and show us the way.

—*Chinook Blessing Litany*

## August 3

There is a woman, Mother of Creation.
She has a child, she is fertile.
I am seed, I've not known where to go
but she has caught me and put me where I belong.

I am here to serve my purpose
I am here to listen to my mother
I am here to be your lover
I am here to beget daughters.

The winds have blown me all about
I can see how weak I am
The winds have blown me everywhere
I know how strong I am.

The seed so weak, the seed so strong, is ready.
Dare I land?
    Mother of Creation, hold me
    —plant me warm and softly in yourself.

Let the miracle of life unfold
Let the moisture of your garden feed
Let the warmth within your bosom flow
    —feed me, Mother of Creation
    I will always love you.

And when I grow I will remember
Just how much I need you, as flower needs the rain

and *you* are rain and sun and wind,
    and you are earth

And as a mother feeds her child,
so the child feeds the mother
for all is of the same food...Love.

Mother of Creation, Love me, I Love you.

Your love is my existence,
My existence is your love.

Mother of Creation, sometimes I think I see
how I try to master you
    as a fool, who tries to catch the sea.

Sometimes I think I see, how the master sets us free
Mother and child adrift upon an ocean
made of three...

    guided by the father, nurtured by the mother
    Give birth to yonder child

    I can hear him crying
    he is father, mother, child
    he is children of creation
    he is you and he is me
    he is all things that we thought we were
    he is all things that we hoped we'd be
    he is you and he is me
    and the father is a child
    and so too, are mothers born.

Mother of Creation, all things pour forth from you
God is father, you are Mother
Inseparably united, you are each other's halves
We are your children. Thank you for giving birth to us.
We are fathers and mothers in turn
And to carry out your will is our command.

Could my mother only see me now,
a sad and broken man
Ah but would she look tomorrow it is sure she'd
understand
how child goes through the pains of birth
until he holds within his hand
the seed to make another man.

Mother of Creation, watch your children grow
Let them fly away on tender wings
you and they will always know
they will return, they cannot go.
Two things cleaved from the same thing
can but forever be the same.

Two souls united in a seed
Give birth to one, the *same.*

All is One beyond the gates of
    Mother of Creation.

Mother—teach us.

—*Tony Basilio*

**August 4**

Hold on to what is good
    Even if it is a handful of earth
Hold on to what you believe
    Even if it is a tree that stands by itself
Hold on to what you must do
    Even if it is a long way from here
Hold on to life
    Even if it is easier to let go
Hold on to my hand
    Even if I have gone away from you

      —*Pueblo blessing*

**August 5**

I asked for strength that I might achieve;
I was made weak that I might learn humbly to obey.

I asked for health that I might do greater things;
I was given infirmity that I might do better things.

I asked for riches that I might be happy;
I was given poverty that I might be wise.

I asked for power that I might have the praise of men;
I was given weakness that I might feel the need of
    God.

I asked for all things that I might enjoy life;
I was given life that I might enjoy all things.

I got nothing that I had asked for,
but everything that I had hoped for.
Almost despite myself my unspoken prayers were
    answered;
I am, among all men, most richly blessed.

*—Prayer of an unknown*
*Confederate soldier*

## August 6

All that we ought to have
    thought and have not thought,
All that we ought to have said, and
    have not said,
All that we ought to have done, and
    have not done;

All that we ought not to have thought,
    and yet have thought,
All that we ought not to have spoken,
    and yet have spoken,
All that we ought not to have done,
    and yet have done;
For thoughts, words and works,
    pray we, O God, for forgiveness.

*—Persian prayer*

## August 7

Health is easy to keep,
Difficult to restore;
Emotions move easily
When first they arise,
Become pain when suppressed;
To respond and release
Means less toil later.

An armored heart is easily injured
And pursuing fantasy invites despair;
A great life is composed of many details,
So walk firmly—each step counts.

A grand canyon began as a tiny cleft
A great master was born a small babe;
Be happy in your place,
Growth is inevitable.
Your start and finish are the same:
The journey to enlightenment begins
Where you are right now.

One who controls
Will be out of control
And the competitive spirit
Is ever wanting.
The sage does not control
And maintains perfect balance;

She does not grab for power
So overflows with it.

The only treasure the master seeks
Is a peaceful heart;
Her only goal
To be full where she is.
Her only doctrine
To allow.

By returning to her origins,
She brings us all forward.

—*Haven Treviño*

### August 8

Dear God,
Please awaken me from this dream.
I fear and I choose not to,
I suffer and I choose not to.
I claim for myself Your resurrection within me,
    my perfect health, my perfect healing, my
      perfect Self in whom there is no pain or fear.
Every cell of my being is radiant with my love for You.
May my earthly self align with this,
May my human heart stop beating so wildly.
May I remember, dear God, that I live in Your mind
and I belong in Your arms.

For there I am healed, and there I am whole.
You are my divine physician.
You know my terror, although it is not real.
You understand my pain, although it is not
    understandable.
You answer with Your spirit.
Dear Lord, please heal me.
I surrender this as I surrender all things
I trust in You in this and all things
I need You, Lord, in this and all things.
Please, dear God.
Amen.

—*Marianne Williamson*

## August 9

We pray for the power to be gentle; the strength to be forgiving; the patience to be understanding; and the endurance to accept the consequences to holding to what we believe to be right.

May we put our trust in the power of good to overcome evil and the power of love to overcome hatred. We pray for the vision to see and the faith to believe in a world emancipated from violence, a new world where fear shall no longer lead men to commit injustice, nor selfishness make them bring suffering to others.

Help us to devote our whole life and thought and energy to the task of making peace, praying always for the inspiration and the power to fulfill the destiny for which we were created.

*—Adapted prayer from Week of Prayer for World Peace, 1978*

### August 10

I salute you, Glorious Virgin, star more brilliant than the sun, redder than the freshest rose, whiter than any lily, higher in heaven than any of the saints. The whole earth reveres you, accept my praise and come to my aid. In the midst of your so glorious days in heaven, do not forget the miseries of this earth; turn your gaze of kindness on all those who suffer and struggle and whose lips are soaked in the bitterness of this life. Have pity on those who loved each other and were torn apart. Have pity on the loneliness of the heart, on the feebleness of our faith, on the objects of our tenderness. Have pity on those who weep, on those who pray, on those who tremble. Give everyone hopefulness and peace.

*—Ancient prayer of protection translated by Andrew Harvey*

## August 11

May beings all live happily and safe
And may their hearts rejoice within themselves.
Whatever there may be with breath of life,
Whether they be frail or very strong,
Without exception, be they long or short
Or middle-sized, or be they big or small,
Or thick, or visible, or invisible,
Or whether they dwell far or they dwell near,
Those that are here, those seeking to exist—
May beings all rejoice within themselves.
Let no one bring about another's ruin
And not despise in any way or place,
Let them not wish each other any ill
From provocation or from enmity.

—*The Buddha*

## August 12

Here we are, God—a planet at prayer. Attune our spirits that we may hear your harmonies and bow before
your creative power
that we may face our violent discords and join with
your Energy
to make heard in every heart your hymn of peace.

Here we are, God—a militarized planet. Transform our fears that we may transform our war fields into wheatfields, arms into handshakes, missiles into messengers of peace.

Here we are, God—a polluted planet. Purify our vision that we may perceive ways to purify our beloved lands, cleanse our precious waters, de-smog our life-giving air.

Here we are, God—an exploited planet. Heal our heart, that we may respect our resources, hold priceless our people, and provide for our starving children an abundance of daily bread.

*—Joan Metzner*

### August 13

This is a prayer for
the illumination of the body
    the body of the earth
    which is our rock and breath
    the body of the self
        which is the shining
        eternal strand of
        the soul
    the body of material substance which
        is the ancient gentle
        temple of the spirit.

May you move your divine hand
across us in each of these planes,
allowing the earth
of our bodies
and the ether
of our souls
to become fit grand vessels
for your and our own
illustrious light.

—*Daphne Rose Kingma*

## August 14

When I walk through thy woods,
may my right foot and my left foot
be harmless to the little creatures
that move in its grasses: as it is said
by the mouth of thy prophet,
They shall not hurt nor destroy
in all my holy mountain.

—*Rabbi Moshe Hakotun*

## August 15

Just give me this:
A rinsing out, a cleansing free of all my smaller
    strivings
So I can be the class act God intended,
True to my purpose,
All my energy aligned behind my deepest intention.

And just this:
A quieting down, a clearing away of internal ruckus,
So I can hear the huge stillness in my heart
And feel
How I pulse with all creation,
Part and parcel of Your great singing ocean.

And this, too:
A willingness to notice and forgive the myriad times
I fall short,
Forgetting who I really am,
What I really belong to.

So I can start over,
Fresh and clean
Like sweet sheets billowing in the summer sun,
My heart pierced with gratitude.

—*Belleruth Naparstek*

## August 16

I am here abroad,
I am here in need,
I am here in pain,
I am here in straits,
I am here alone.
O God, aid me.

—*Celtic charm*

## August 17

Pain is the great teacher. I woke before dawn with this thought. Joy, happiness, are what we take and do not question. They are beyond question, maybe. A matter of being. But pain forces us to think, and to make connections, to sort out what is what, to discover what has been happening to cause it. And, curiously enough, pain draws us to other human beings in a significant way, whereas joy or happiness to some extent, isolates.

—*May Sarton*

## August 18

*In 1920, the 19th Amendment*
*to the U.S. Constitution is*
*ratified, giving women the*
*right to vote*

When I think of peace, I think of a world where human beings are no longer brutalized on account of such accidents of birth as sex, race, religion, or nationality. For me, peace is a way of structuring human relations where daily acts of kindness and caring are tangibly rewarded. It is a way of thinking, feeling, and acting where our essential interconnection with one another is truly honored.

I pray for a world where we live in partnership rather than domination; where "man's conquest of nature" is recognized as suicidal and sacrireligious; where power is no longer equated with the blade, but with the holy chalice: the ancient symbol of the power to give, nurture, enhance life. And I not only pray, but actively work, for the day when it will be so.

—*Riane Eisler*


## August 19

Grant, O my Savior, that I may observe, with the greatest care, Thy precept of charity towards my neighbor, to love him as Thou hast loved us, since this is absolutely necessary for salvation. Give me also that tenderness of charity which may prevent me from wounding it in any way: for Thou hast said that to offend our neighbor is to wound the apple of Thine eye. Grant, therefore, that I may avoid Thy displeasure by not incurring the displeasure of my neighbor.

*—Thomas à Kempis*

## August 20

O Heart of Love,
I put all my trust in you.
For I fear all things from my own weakness,
but I hope for all things from your goodness.

Had I a thousand bodies, O my God, a thousand loves and a thousand lives, I would immolate them all to Your service.

*—Saint Margaret Mary Alacoque*

## August 21

Heavenly Father, charge my body with Thy vitality, charge my mind with Thy spiritual power, charge my soul with Thy joy, Thine immortality.

*—Yogananda,*
*Metaphysical Meditations*

**August 22**

We join with the earth and with each other.

To bring new life to the land
To restore the waters
To refresh the air

We join with the earth and with each other.

To renew the forests
To care for the plants
To protect the creatures

We join with the earth and with each other.

To celebrate the seas
To rejoice in the sunlight
To sing the song of the stars

We join with the earth and with each other.

To recreate the human community
To promote justice and peace
To remember our children

We join with the earth and with each other.

We join together as many and diverse expressions
of one loving mystery: for the healing of the earth and
the renewal of all life.

—*U.N. Environmental Sabbath Program*

**August 23**

We go beyond the veil of fear,
lighting each other's way.
The holiness that leads us
is within us, as is our home.

> —*From A Course in Miracles*
> *(Text, page 399)*

**August 24**

Resurrection. The reversal of what was thought to be absolute. The turning of midnight into dawn, hatred into love, dying into living anew.

If we look more closely into life, we will find that resurrection is more than hope, it is our experience. The return to life from death is something we understand at our innermost depths, something we feel on the surface of our tender skin. We have come back to life, not only when we start to shake off a shroud of sorrow that has bound us, but when we begin to believe in all that is still, endlessly possible.

We give thanks for all those times we have arisen from the depths or simply taken a tiny step toward something new. May we be empowered by extraordinary second chances. And as we enter the world anew, let us turn the tides of despair into endless waves of hope.

> —*Molly Fumia*

## August 25

Let not your hearts be troubled, neither let them be afraid.

—*John 14:27*

## August 26

Divine Mother, Father God, absolute source of my existence, cure the root cause of all my suffering—spiritual ignorance. Awaken within my physical body, spine, and brain the memory of divinity—my soul's true nature.

Lead my consciousness from the outer deceptive ever-changing light and shadows of the physical world to that which alone is Real—the inner unchanging pure Light and joy of my soul.

Help me to realize that present within this body temple is Your unconditional healing love waiting for my heart and mind's recognition. Help your child to become the fully healed and immortal Being you created me to be.

—*Judith Cornell*

**August 27**

*Albanian-born
Indian missionary
Mother Teresa
is born in 1910*

Make us worthy, Lord,
 to serve others throughout the world
  who live and die
   in poverty or hunger,
Give them, through our hands, this day their daily
bread,
 and by our understanding love,
  give peace and joy.

    —*Mother Teresa*

**August 28**

*In 1963, Martin
Luther King, Jr.,
delivers this
speech in
Washington, DC*

I have a dream today.
I have a dream that one day every valley shall be
 exalted,

every hill and mountain shall be made low,
and the crooked places will be made straight,
and the glory of the Lord shall be revealed,
and all flesh shall see it together.

This is our hope. This is the faith with which I return.

With this faith we will be able to hew out of the
mountain of despair
a stone of hope.

With this faith we will be able to transform the jan
gling discords of our nation
into a beautiful symphony of brotherhood.

With this faith we will be able to work together, to
pray together, to struggle together, to go to jail
together, to stand up for freedom together,
knowing we will be free one day.

This will be the day when all of God's children will be
able to sing with a new meaning

My country, 'tis of thee
Sweet land of liberty,
Of thee I sing:
Land where my fathers died,
Land of the pilgrim's pride,
From every mountain-side
Let freedom ring.

And if America is to be a great nation this must
become true.

So let freedom ring from the prodigious hilltops of
New Hampshire.

Let freedom ring from the mighty mountains of
New York.
Let freedom ring from the heightening Alleghenies of
Pennsylvania!
Let freedom ring from the snowcapped Rockies of
Colorado!
Let freedom ring from the curvaceous peaks of
California!
But not only that; let freedom ring from Stone
Mountain of Georgia!
Let freedom ring from Lookout Mountain of
Tennessee!
Let freedom ring from every hill and molehill of
Mississippi.
From every mountainside, let freedom ring.
When we let freedom ring, when we let it ring
from every village and every hamlet, from every state
and every city,
we will be able to speed up the day when all of God's
children,
black men and white men, Jews and Gentiles,
Protestants and Catholics,
will be able to join hands and sing in the words of the
old Negro spiritual,
"Free at last! thank God almighty, we are free at last!"

—*Martin Luther King, Jr.*

**August 29**

> Bless all people; pray for their happiness, joy, and
> laughter.

> —*From the Vedic Scriptures*

**August 30**

> May it be delightful my house;
> From my head may it be delightful;
> To my feet may it be delightful;
> Where I lie may it be delightful;
> All above me may it be delightful;
> All around me may it be delightful.

> —*Navaho chant*

**August 31**

> It seems to me that the whole secret of life, if it is to
> be happy, is in the spirit of love; and when an old
> form of love dies we must take on the new. If life is to
> be made interesting and worth its breath, we must
> look on ourselves as growing children, right up to the
> end of our days.

> —*W.H. Davies*

## September 1

You hear the long roll of the plunging ground,
The whistle of stones, the quail's cry in the grass.
I stammer like a bird, I rasp like stone,
I mutter, with gray hands upon my face.
The earth blurs, beyond me, into dark.
Spinning in such bewildered sleep, I need
To know you, whirring above me, when I wake.
Come down. Come down. I lie afraid.
I have lain alien in my self so long,
How can I understand love's angry tongue?

> —*James Wright,*
> *"A Prayer in My Sickness"*

## September 2

O my God, come to me, so that You may dwell in me
and I may dwell in you.

> —*Saint John Vianney*

**September 3**

Spirit, grant me:
The vision and wisdom of the elder she-eagle
The fierce focus of the lioness
The fluid leadership of wild geese
Small creatures' ways of stillness
Beaver's strong and beautiful cozy lodge
The devotion of a dearly beloved loyal dog.

Fill my spirit with the wild abandon-infused
winds of autumn that keep positive and
negative space moving and changing,
charged and clear.
Fill my inner circle with the Beloved in the
form of lover, partner, true friends, family,
truth and laughter.

May my work reflect the light and the
shadows that are my being.
May I have clarity.
May I know when and where to begin and
when and how to stop.
May I always have the strength to ask the
hard question,
to peer deeply into the dark pools,
the patience to wait for sediment to clear.

—*Marcy Tilton,*
*"Artist's Prayer"*

### September 4

Give me strength to refrain from the unkind silence
that is born of hardness of heart; the unkind silence
that clouds the serenity of understanding and is the
enemy of peace.

Give me strength to be the first to tender the
healing word and the renewal of friendship, that the
bonds of amity and the flow of charity may be
strengthened.

—*Cecil Hunt*


### September 5

Now I pray that each and every being's true nature be
revealed, that we each see clearly our inherent truth
and find liberation from the shackles of suffering and
difficulty imposed by the limitations of our mind.

—*Chagdud Tulku*


### September 6

Lord, your harvest is the harvest of love;
love sown in the hearts of people;
love that spreads out
like the branches of a great tree
covering all who seek its shelter;

love that inspires and recreates;
love that is planted in the weak and the weary;
the sick and the dying.
The harvest of your love is the life that reaches
through the weeds of sin and death
to the sunlight of resurrection.
Lord, nurture my days with your love,
water my soul with the dew of forgiveness,
that the harvest of my life might be your joy.

—*Frank Topping*

## September 7

*In 1892, U.S.*
*poet John Greenleaf*
*Whittier dies*

Drop thy still dews of quietness
    Till our all striving cease;
Take from our souls the strain and stress,
And let our ordered lives confess
    The beauty of thy peace.

—*John Greenleaf Whittier*

## September 8

> May I become a medicine for the sick and their
> physician, their support until sickness come not again.
> May I become an unfailing store for the wretched,
> and be first to supply them with their needs.
> My own self and my pleasures, my righteousness
> past, present and future, may I sacrifice without
> regard, in order to achieve the welfare of beings.

—Santideva

## September 9

God my Father,

I thank You that You are love, the only power in
the world, all-powerful and omnipresent. I thank You
for making me, Your beloved child, in Your own image.
I am made in the image of the great Creator of the
universe and of His own substance, created of Love and
in its image, a substance that cannot deteriorate.

I ask Your comfort, protection and healing for
myself and for all Your children who are in need. I ask
that You give me firm guidance that I cannot fail to
understand, to show me how to simplify my activities
and possessions, to be rid of all that are inessential or
which reflect my low self-esteem. I ask You to guide
me to simplify my diet as well. If there are activities
that could bring about my healing, I ask this guidance

as well. Nothing You guide me to do will be seen as so inconsequential that it cannot effect a cure.

As I obey and as I forgive others, I will receive my healing. If I have repressed memories and emotions, I ask that they be brought to light so that my healing will be lasting. I thank You in advance for your mighty healing power, and I will tell the world how You healed me. I ask that Your glory may shine in me as I give up all evidence of disease. I will show the world that I am indeed of God and under His protection. Amen.

—*Martha Anne Sorenson*

### September 10

Forgive me, most gracious Lord and Father, if this day I have done or said anything to increase the pain of the world. Pardon the unkind word, the impatient gesture, the hard and selfish deed, the failure to show sympathy and kindly help where I have had the opportunity but missed it; and enable me so to live that I may daily do something to lessen the tide of human sorrow, and add to the sum of human happiness.

—*Christian, date unknown*

## September 11

Never a trial that
　　He is not there.
Never a burden that
　　He does not bear.
Never a sorrow that
　　He does not share.
Moment by moment
　　I'm under His care.

—D. W. Whittle

## September 12
*South African civil rights
leader Steven Biko dies in
jail in 1977*

We regard our living together not as an unfortunate
　　mishap
warranting endless competition among us
but as a deliberate act of God
to make us a community of brothers and sisters
jointly involved in the quest for a composite answer
to the varied problems of life.

—*Steven Biko*

## September 13

O Hidden Life, vibrant in every atom,
O Hidden Light, shining in every creature,
O Hidden Love, embracing all in Oneness,
May we each who feels himself as one with Thee
Know he is therefore one with every other.

—*Annie Besant*

## September 14

Lead me to places of loneliness and pain.
May Your words shine in my mouth.
May I trust that the way You have made me
is the way that is needed.

—*Rachel Naomi Remen, M.D.*

## September 15

O Brightness of brightness, o clearness of clear!
Aisling★ of vision in my heart appear.
Blessed your fragrance, your grace is the dew
That on my soul falling shall heal me anew.

—*Caitlin Matthews*

(★Aisling, pronounced *esh-ling,* is a Gaelic term for a vision)

**September 16**

I can be hurt by nothing but my thoughts.

*—From A Course in Miracles*
*(Workbook, page 428)*


**September 17**

With my sacred power, I am traveling.
With my sacred power, I am traveling.
With my sacred power, I am traveling.

At the back of my house, white shell prayer offerings
are placed;
    they are beautifully decorated;
  With my sacred power, I am traveling,
At the center of my house, turquoise prayer offerings
are placed;
    they are beautifully decorated;
  With my sacred power, I am traveling,
In my house by the fireside, abalone prayer offerings
are placed;
    they are beautifully decorated;
  With my sacred power I am traveling,
In my house, in the corners by the door,
    black jewel prayer offerings are placed;
  With my sacred power, I am traveling,

In the doorway of my house, rock crystal prayer
offerings are placed;
    they are beautifully decorated;
  With my sacred power, I am traveling.
All about my house is Talking God; He is
beautifully clad;
  With my sacred power, I am traveling.
All about my house is Hogan God; She is
beautifully clad;
  With my sacred power, I am traveling.
All about my house, bushes are growing;
    they are beautifully leafed out;
  With my sacred power, I am traveling.
All about my house, trees are growing;
    they are beautifully leafed out;
  With my sacred power, I am traveling.
All about my house, rocks are standing;
    their surfaces are beautiful;
  With my sacred power, I am traveling.
All about my house, mountains are standing;
    their sides are beautiful;
  With my sacred power, I am traveling.
All about my house, springs are flowing; they are
beautiful;
  With my sacred power, I am traveling.
All about my house is White Corn Boy; He is
beautifully clad;
  With my sacred power, I am traveling.

All about my house is Yellow Corn Girl; She is
beautifully clad;
   With my sacred power, I am traveling.
All about my house is Corn Pollen Boy; He is
beautifully clad;
   With my sacred power, I am traveling.
All about my house is Corn Beetle Girl; She is
beautifully clad;
   With my sacred power, I am traveling.
With beauty before me, I am traveling,

   With my sacred power I am traveling,
With beauty behind me, I am traveling,
   With my sacred power, I am traveling,
With beauty below me, I am traveling,
   With my sacred power, I am traveling,
With beauty above me, I am traveling,
   With my sacred power, I am traveling,
Now with long life, now with everlasting beauty, I live.
   I am traveling,
   With my sacred power, I am traveling,

   With my sacred power, I am traveling,
   With my sacred power, I am traveling,
   With my sacred power, I am traveling, it is said.

*—Navaho, date unknown*
*(Blessing Way for a*
*girl's puberty rites)*

## September 18

May you be for us a moon of joy and happiness. Let the young become strong and the grown man maintain his strength, the pregnant woman be delivered and the woman who has given birth suckle her child. Let the stranger come to the end of his journey and those who remain at home dwell safely in their houses. Let the flocks that go to feed in the pastures return happily. May you be a moon of harvest and of calves. May you be a moon of restoration and of good health.

*—Mensa, Ethiopia*

## September 19

Follow diligently the Way in your own heart, but make no display of it to the world. Keep behind, and you shall be put in front; keep out, and you shall be kept in. He that humbles himself shall be preserved entire. He that bends shall be made straight. He that is empty shall be filled. He that is worn out shall be renewed.

*—Lao-Tzu*

## September 20

> God, Let there be awareness
>> where ignorance now prevails.
> Scatter our long hidden fears
>> with your bright beam of courage.
> And knit fine cloaks of your love
>> to shelter us and the world.

> —*Debbie Aliya*

## September 21
*Rosh Hashanah*
*(date varies)*

> Today, today, today. Bless us . . .
> and help us to grow.

> —*From the Rosh Hashanah liturgy*

AUTUMN

**September 22**

*Autumnal Equinox*

> The summer yields to the autumn winds blowing
> While the cool burns the leaves golden red
> We harvest fields we planted once knowing
> Grains of truth would soon come to a head.
>
> Mystery Healer, I feel your hand above my brow
> Into your love I bow.
>
> Aging dreams seeming hard to remember
> Alluring sleep ever taking its toll
> Love redeems like the snows of December
> Pure and deep as the infinite soul.
>
> Mystery Healer, I feel your hand above my brow
> Into your love I bow.
>
> To meadowlands of our soul's flowering
> We return from the roots we have sprung
> To understand love we know is empowering
> Though we learn from the truth where love hung.
>
> Mystery Healer, I feel your hand above my brow
> Into your love I bow.

> —*Chris Van Cleave*

## September 23

Would it not take one
Who slept alone to know it?
Who could have told you
That the nights in autumn
Are indeed extremely long?

—*Takashina Kishi*

## September 24

May creatures all abound in weal and peace
May all be blessed with peace always.
Let none cajole or flout
His fellow anywhere
Let none wish others harm
In dudgeon or hate.
Just as with her own life, a mother
Shields from hurt her own, her only child,
Let all-embracing thoughts
For all that lives be thine—
An all-embracing love for all the universe
In all its heights and depths and breadth,
Unstinted love, unmarred by hate within . . .

—*The Sutta Nipata Sutra*

## September 25

Almighty God, who are mother and father to us all,
Look upon your planet Earth divided:
Help us to know that we are all your children;
That all nations belong to one great family,
And all of our religions lead to you.

Multiply our prayers in every land
Until the whole Earth becomes your congregation,
United in your love.
Sustain our vision of a peaceful future
And give us strength to work unceasingly
To make that vision real. Amen.

—*Helen Weaver*

## September 26
*U.S.-born British poet
and playwright T.S. Eliot
is born in 1888*

Blessèd sister, holy mother, spirit of the fountain,
    spirit of the garden,
Suffer us not to mock ourselves with falsehood
Teach us to care and not to care
Teach us to sit still
Even among these rocks.
Our peace in His will

And even among these rocks
Sister, mother,
And spirit of the river, spirit of the sea.,
Suffer me not to be separated

And let my cry come unto Thee.

—*T.S. Eliot*

## September 27

Oh God, whose vast light devours all differences and in whose majesty all prejudices tremble, we pray for an opening of our hearts to all our gay brothers and sisters. We ask you to break down the walls that divide us, that keep us estranged.

Give us compassion for the sufferings they have suffered, violations of the spirit through prejudice, discrimination, and judgment, a plague of illness and death; and may we honor them for the bountiful gifts they have brought us, gifts that expand and nourish our spirits.

We acknowledge the burden they have carried in being the living embodiment of the blending of the male and female energies, and give thanks for their living out of the message that human essence is not of the body but of the spirit, not of gender but of consciousness, not of prejudice but of great love.

—*Daphne Rose Kingma*

## September 28

When I rise up
let me rise up joyful
like a bird

When I fall
let me fall without regret
like a leaf

—*Wendell Berry*

## September 29

Be patient with everyone, but above all with yourself . . . do not be disheartened by your imperfections,
but always rise up with fresh courage. How are we
to be patient in dealing with our neighbor's faults if
we are impatient in dealing with our own? They who
are fretted by their own failings will not correct them.
All profitable correction comes from a calm and
peaceful mind.

—*Saint Francis de Sales*

## September 30
*Yom Kippur*
*(date varies)*

> Evening, and morning, and at noon will I pray, and cry
> aloud: and he shall hear my voice.
>
> —*Psalm 55:17*

## October 1

> O God who art Peace everlasting, whose chosen
> reward is the gift of peace, and who has taught us
> that the peacemakers are Thy children, pour Thy sweet
> peace into our souls, that everything discordant may
> utterly vanish, and all that makes for peace be sweet
> for us forever.
>
> —*Galasian*

## October 2

> May everyone be happy and safe, and may their
>   hearts be filled with joy.
>
> May all living beings live in Security and in Peace—
> beings who are frail or strong, tall or short, big or
> small, visible or not visible, near or far away,
> already born or yet to be born.
> May all of them dwell in perfect tranquility.

Let no one do harm to anyone. Let no one put the life of anyone in danger. Let no one, out of anger or ill will, wish anyone any harm.

—*Metta Sutta (Suttanipata)*
*Translated by Thich Nhat Hanh*

## October 3

You are ever mighty,
Lord Who brings the dead to life,
You are great in granting salvation,
providing the living with sustenance with loving-kindness,
bringing the dead to life with great mercies,
supporting the fallen,
healing the sick,
releasing the captive,
and keeping faith with those asleep in the dust.
Who is like You, Master of mighty acts,
and who compares to You,
King Who causes death and restores lif
and causes salvation to sprout?
And You are faithful to bring the dead to life.
Blessed are You,
Lord Who brings the dead to life.

—*Traditional prayer from*
*the Jewish daily liturgy*

## October 4

*Saint Francis of Assisi*
*is born in 1181 or 1182*

> Lord make me an instrument of Your peace.
> where there is hatred, let me sow love;
> where there is injury, pardon;
> where there is doubt, faith;
> where there is darkness, light;
> and where there is sadness, joy.
> O Divine Master, grant that I may not
> so much seek to be consoled as to console;
> to be understood as to understand;
> to be loved as to love,
> For it is in giving that we receive,
> it is in pardoning that we are pardoned,
> and it is in dying that we are born to eternal life.

> —*Saint Francis of Assisi*

## October 5

> O Lord, remember not only the men and women
> of good will, but also those of ill will. But do not
> remember all the suffering they have inflicted on us;
> remember the fruits we have bought, thanks to this
> suffering—our comradeship, our loyalty, our humility,
> our courage, our generosity, the greatness of heart
> which has grown out of all this, and when they come

to judgement let all the fruits which we have borne be their forgiveness.

—*An unknown prisoner in*
*Ravensbruck concentration camp*

## October 6

Holy Spirit,
giving life to all life,
moving all creatures,
root of all things,
washing them clean,
wiping out their mistakes,
healing their wounds,
you are our true life,
luminous, wonderful,
awakening the heart
from its ancient sleep.

—*Hildegard of Bingen*
*Translated by Stephen Mitchell*

## October 7

To forgive our brother is to forgive
Ourselves—
We abandon our revenge;
Our lives have seen suffering enough.

We are tired and worn out with
Ourselves—

If I take revenge, it will be the cause;
The effect will follow me into my next life.
Look into the mirror; see the compassion
     in your heart.
Avoid all resentment and hatred for Mankind.

—*Le Ly Hayslip*

### October 8

Great Spirit, whose dry lands thirst, help us to find
the way to refresh your lands.

We pray for your power to refresh your lands.

Great Spirit, whose waters are choked with debris and
pollution, help us to find the way to cleanse your
waters.

We pray for your knowledge to find the way to
cleanse the waters.

Great Spirit, whose beautiful earth grows ugly with
misuse, help us to find the way to restore beauty to
your handiwork.

We pray for your strength to restore the beauty of
your handiwork.

Great Spirit, whose creatures are being destroyed,
help us to find a way to replenish them.

We pray for your power to replenish the earth.

Great Spirit, whose gifts to us are being lost in
selfishness and corruption, help us to find the
way to restore our humanity.

We pray for your wisdom to find the way to restore
our humanity.

*—U.N. Environmental*
*Sabbath Program*

### October 9

If I could see you, Spirit,
all of the time
I would ask myself
then how would I act or think or be.
Let me begin to believe
that you are in the front of my eyes
and in the back of my mind,

witnessing every thought,
every word,
every endeavor
... for you are.

—*Diane Cirincione*

### October 10

Fill your bowl to the brim
and it will spill.
Keep sharpening your knife
and it will blunt.
Chase after money and security
and your heart will never unclench.
Care about people's approval
and you will be their prisoner.

Do your work, then step back.
The only path to serenity.

—*Lao-Tzu*
*Translated by*
*Stephen Mitchell*

## October 11

O God, Who by the grace of the Holy Ghost hast
poured the gifts of love into our hearts; Grant unto my
friends and kindred, especially [names] health of body
and soul, and every spiritual gift; that they may love
Thee with all their strength, and with perfect affection
fulfill Thy pleasure.

—*Christian, date unknown*

226

## October 12

I love to watch how birds
    soar on the wind.
There appears to be such
    little effort, yet such joy.

I want to become like a bird
    and let my spirit soar
on the winds that are blowing
    through my life.

I will not be crushed against
    the rocks!
I will sense the rhythm, the
    flow, and react accordingly.
I will trust my inner guide.

—*Judith Garrett Garrison*
*and Scott Sheperd*

## October 13

All beauty warms the heart, is a sign of health, prosperity and the favour of God. What delights, what emancipates, not what scares and pains us, is wise and good in speech and in the arts. For, truly, the heart at the centre of the universe with every throb hurls the flood of happiness into every artery, vein, and veinlet, so that the whole system is inundated with the tides of joy.

—*Ralph Waldo Emerson*

## October 14

First you must love your body, in games
in wild places, in bodies of others,
Then you must enter the world of men and
learn all worldly ways. You must sicken.
You must return to your Mother and notice
how quiet the house is.
Then return to the world that is
not Man
that you may finally walk in the
world of Man, speaking.

—*Lew Welch*

## October 15

*German philosopher*
*Friedrich Wilhelm*
*Nietzche is born*
*in 1844*

Remain faithful to the earth, my brothers and sisters, with the power of your virtue. Let your gift-giving love and your knowledge serve the meaning of the earth. Thus I beg and beseech you. Do not let them fly away from earthly things and beat with their wings against eternal walls. Alas, there has always been so much virtue that has flown away. Lead back to the earth the virtue that flew away... back to the body, back to life, that it may give the earth a meaning...

Verily, the earth shall yet become a site of recovery. And even now a new fragrance surrounds it, bringing salvation—and a new hope.

*—Friedrich Nietzsche*

## October 16

I am not I.
   I am this one
walking beside me whom I do not see,
whom at times I manage to visit,
and whom at other times I forget;
who remains calm and silent while I talk,

and forgives, gently, when I hate,
who walks where I am not,
who will remain standing when I die.

> —*Juan Ramon Jimenez*
> *Translated by Robert Bly*

### October 17

Let Reality govern my every thought, and Truth be the
heart of my life.
For so it must be for all of humanity. Please help me to
do "my part."
And may the intensity of all our egos become the Joy
of our One Soul!

> —*Adapted from The Tibetan's*
> *teachings in the Alice Bailey*
> *materials by Jacquelyn Small*

### October 18

I come before thee as one of thy many children. See, I
am small and weak; I need thy strength and wisdom.

Grant me to walk in beauty and that my eyes may ever
behold the crimson sunset. May my hands treat
with respect the things which thou hast created,
may my ears hear thy voice!

Make me wise, that I may understand the things which
thou hast taught my people, which thou hast
hidden in every leaf and every rock.

I long for strength, not in order that I may overreach
my brother but to fight my greatest enemy—
myself.

Make me ever ready to come to thee with pure hands
and candid eyes, so that my spirit, when life disappears like the setting sun, may stand unashamed
before thee.

*—Sioux prayer*

### October 19

Yes, Lord, if it please you, cure me. I will not refuse any
work. If I can be of service to a few souls, grant, O
Lord, by the intercession of Your most holy Mother, to
return to me o such health as will not be contrary to
the welfare of my soul.

*—Saint John (Don) Bosco*

### October 20

I do not ask to walk smooth paths
nor bear an easy load.

I pray for strength and fortitude
to climb the rock strewn road.

Give me such courage and I can scale
the headiest peaks alone,
And transform every stumbling block
into a stepping stone.

—*Gail Brook Burket*

## October 21

Godness, You who created our bodies and our minds,
I (We) come to you now, trusting Your healing
    presence.
It is You who fashioned our organs, bones, tissues
    and cells
To work together in harmony for Your eternal
    purpose.
There is no disorder in You and your pattern for us is
    perfect.
Yet, in this world, dis-ease disrupts Your will for us.

We confess we have misused the earth
And this misuse impacts our bodies.
We confess we misuse our emotions, minds and
    spirits,
And this misuse brings pain and disruption to our
    lives.

Forgive us now for our wrongful use of Your gifts.
Restore us by your love to full harmony with Your
    perfect plan.

We know dis-ease is not Your will for us.
Your love is unconditional. Yet, pain is our teacher.
Open us to listen that we may again align ourselves
    with You.
Where we are unable to restore the earth to its
    perfection,
When we are unable to root out our mistakes of body
    and mind,
Nevertheless, be kind to us. Count our fumbling
    efforts as sufficient.

Restore us now to full health,
According to Thy desire for us.
Bring harmony to our lives,
To body, mind, and spirit.
We thank you now, trusting
Your love to bring our healing.

—*Arlene E. Swanson*

**October 22**

Whatever house I enter,
I shall come to heal.

—*The Hippocratic Oath*

## October 23

Eternal wellspring of peace—
May we be drenched with the longing for peace
that we may give ourselves over to peace
until the earth overflows with peace
as living waters overflow the seas.

—*Marcia Falk*

## October 24

*British poet*
*Denise Levertov*
*is born in 1923*

As swimmers dare
to lie face to the sky
and water bears them,
as hawks rest upon air
and air sustains them,
so would I learn to attain
freefall, and float
into Creator Spirit's deep embrace,
knowing no effort earns
that all-surrounding grace.

—*Denise Levertov*

**October 25**

O Great Spirit, whose care reaches to the uttermost
parts of the earth; we humbly beseech thee to behold
and bless those whom we love, nowabsent from us, and
defend them from all dangers of soul and body.

—*Adapted from The Book
of Common Prayer*

**October 26**

May we live our lives beyond separation, knowing that
nations and cultures are made up of individuals. May I
be as one who rethinks my life, my actions, and aligns
to the glory we are all capable of. May I follow where I
am spiritually guided, and embrace what is new that is
of love. May love flow through me and lend my individual life and light toward a better world.

—*Jacqueline T. Snyder
(Eagle Speaks Woman)*

**October 27**

Heavenly Father, my body cells are made of light, my
fleshly cells are made of Thee. They are Spirit, for Thou
art Spirit; they are immortal, for Thou art Life.

—*Yogananda,
Metaphysical Meditations*

**October 28**

I have tried in every way to be loving,
but my love is a heavy love.
It doesn't really lift me or anybody else up.
I see that's because of my fears,
especially my fear that I am not enough,
so I now ask that these fears be taken from me.

And I ask You to take over—
you, the higher power.
I ask you to run this show for me
from now on, to fill me with light;
I ask you in your higher wisdom
to solve all these problems for me.

I've tried to be as loving as I can,
but I see that despite my best efforts,
my love is a wistful love,
a pained love, a wounded love,
and since I don't know what else to do,
I ask you, God, my higher self,
the highest power in the universe,
to fill me, to guide me,
and to take over.

—*Judy Ford*

## October 29

Hear our humble prayer, O God, for our friends the animals. We entreat for them all thy mercy and pity, and for those who deal with them we ask a heart of compassion and gentle hands and kindly words. Make us ourselves to be true friends to animals and so to share the blessing of the merciful. For the sake of thy Son, the tender-hearted, Jesus Christ our Lord.

236

*—Russian prayer, date unknown*

## October 30

Through the great pain of stretching
beyond all that pain has taught me,
the soft well at the base
has opened, and life
touching me there
has turned me into a flower
that prays for rain.  Now
I understand: to blossom
is to pray, to wilt and shed
is to pray, to turn to mulch
is to pray, to stretch in the dark
is to pray, to break the surface
after great months of ice
is to pray, and to squeeze love

up the stalky center toward the sky
with only dreams of color
is to pray, and finally to unfold
again as if never before
is to be the prayer.

> —*Mark Nepo,*
> *"God's Wounds"*

## October 31

*Halloween*

> May God, like a mother eagle, spread the wings of
> Her love and protection over us throughout this
> night, and forever. Amen.

> —*Marchiene Vroon Rienstra*

## November 1

*All Saint's Day*

> May God bless us not with clean air alone,
> But the will to keep our air clean.

> May God bless us not with a vision of a healthy planet
> alone,
> But with the will to do all in our power to restore and
> maintain our planet's health.

May God bless us not with a change of heart in the
    great world leaders alone to save our planet,
But with a change in our own heart to use our own
    power to save the planet.

May the blessing of God not bring to us saints alone,
But make of us saints greater than any we imagine.

                —*Daniel J. McGill*

**November 2**

Wa-kon'da,
here needy he stands,
and I am he.

           —*Omaha tribal prayer*

**November 3**
*U.S. Election Day*
*(date varies)*

O God, forgive our rich nation where small babies die
    of cold quite legally.

O God, forgive our rich nation where small children
    suffer from hunger quite legally.

O God, forgive our rich nation where toddlers and
    school children die from guns sold quite
    legally.

O God, forgive our rich nation that lets children be
    the poorest group of citizens quite legally.

O God, forgive our rich nation that lets the rich
    continue to get more at the expense of the
    poor quite legally.

O God, forgive our rich nation which thinks security
    rests in missiles rather than in mothers, and
    in bombs rather than in babies.

O God, forgive our rich nation for not giving You
    sufficient thanks by giving to others their
    daily bread.

O God, help us never to confuse what is quite legal
    with what is just and right in Your sight.

    —*Marian Wright Edelman*

## November 4

When the signs of age begin to mark my body
(and still more when they touch my mind);
when the ill that is to diminish me or carry me
    off strikes from without
or is born within me;
when the painful moment comes in which I
    suddenly waken
to the fact that I am ill or growing old;
and above all at the last moment

when I feel I am losing hold of myself
and am absolutely passive in the hands
of the great unknown forces that have formed me;
in all those dark moments, O God,
grant that I may understand that it is you
(provided only my faith is strong enough)
who are painfully parting the fibers of my being
in order to penetrate to the very marrow of my
    substance
and bear me away within yourself.

—*Teilhard de Chardin*

### November 5

Heal me, O Lord, and I shall be healed; Save me, and I
shall be saved: for thou art my praise.

—*The Tanuch/Prophets,
Jeremiah XVII,14*

### November 6

Let us all resolve: First to attain the grace of
silence; Second to deem all fault-finding that does
no good a sin ... Third to practice the grace and
virtue of praise.

—*Harriet Beecher Stowe*

**November 7**

This is how a human being can change:
there's a worm addicted to eating
grape leaves.
        Suddenly, he wakes up,
call it grace, whatever, something
wakes him, and he's no longer
a worm.
        He's the entire vineyard,
and the orchard too, the fruit, the trunks,
a growing wisdom and joy
that doesn't need
to devour.

                —*Rumi*
                *Translated by Coleman Barks*

**November 8**

Let me not pray to be sheltered from dangers
        but to be fearless in facing them.
Let me not beg for the stilling of my pain
        but for the heart to conquer it.
Let me not crave in anxious fear to be saved
        but hope for the patience to win my freedom.

                —*Rabindranath Tagore*

## November 9

We beseech you O Lord, to grant us your help and
protection.

Deliver the afflicted, pity the lowly, raise the
fallen, reveal yourself to the needy, heal the sick, and
bring home your wandering people. Feed the hungry,
ransom the captive, support the weak, comfort the
faint-hearted. Let all the nations of the earth know that
you alone are God, that Jesus Christ is your child and
that we are your people and the sheep of your pasture.

*—Saint Clement of Rome*

## November 10

May peace be with you in heart and mind and body.
May you experience Grace and Healing Love. May you
be lifted as Life opens windows through which the
Eternal sends Light.

*—Annabelle Woodard*

## November 11
*Veteran's Day*

Almighty God, grant us grace fearlessly to contend
against evil, and to make no peace with oppression;
and, that we may reverently use our freedom, help us

to employ it in the maintenance of justice among people and nations.

—Adapted from The Book<br>of Common Prayer

## November 12

O merciful Father, who has given life to many and lovest all that thou has made, give us the spirit of thine own loving kindness that we may show mercy to all helpless creatures. Especially would we pray for those which minister to our sport or comfort, that they may be treated with tenderness of hands, in thankfulness of heart, and that we may discover thee, the Creator, in all created things.

—Christian, date unknown

## November 13

As I travel through my life
Times of joy and times of strife
I pray now to realize
The whole within—energize
My spirit self to align
With Universal All Divine.

—Beverly Shapiro

**November 14**

You are so young, so before all beginning, and I want
to beg you, as much as I can, to be patient toward all
that is unsolved in your heart and to try to love the
questions *themselves* like locked rooms and like books
that are written in a very foreign tongue. Do not now
seek the answers, which cannot be given you because
you would not be able to live them. And the point is,
to love everything. *Live* the questions now. Perhaps you
will then gradually, without noticing it, live along some
distant day into the answer.

Resolve to be always beginning—to be a
beginner!

—*Rainer Maria Rilke*


**November 15**

When we get out of the glass bottles of our ego,
and when we escape like squirrels turning in the
    cages of our personality
and get into the forests again,
we shall shiver with cold and fright
but things will happen to us
so that we don't know ourselves.

Cool, unlying life will rush in,
and passion will make our bodies taut with power,

we shall stamp our feet with new power
and old things will fall down,
we shall laugh, and institutions will curl up like
    burnt paper.

—*D.H. Lawrence*

## November 16

As the sun illuminates
the moon and the stars,
so let us illumine
one another.

—*Anonymous*

## November 17

We seek a renewed stirring of life for the earth
We plead that what we are capable of doing is
not always what we ought to do.
We urge that all people now determine
that a wide untrammeled freedom shall remain
to testify that this generation has love for the next.
If we want to succeed in that, we might show, mean
    while,
a little more love for this one, and for each other.

—*Nancy Newhall*

## November 18

Fear Not.
What is not real, never was and never will be.
What is real, always was and cannot be destroyed.

*—Bhagavad Gita*

## November 19

Hold on in the darkness though no gleam of light
    breaks through.
Keep on dreaming dreams although they never quite
    come true.
Keep on moving forward though you don't know
    what's ahead.
Keep on keeping on though it's a lonely road ahead.

Keep on looking up towards the goal you have in
    view.
Keep on at the task God has given you to do.
Keep on in the hope that there are better times in
    store.
Keep on praying for the thing that you are waiting
    for.

Blessings come to those who in the turmoil of events
Seek to see the goodness of the Will of Providence.
Hold to this and never doubt. Keep head and spirits
    high.

You'll discover that the storm was only passing by.

Seek Love in the pity of another's woe,
In the gentle relief of another's care.
In the darkness of night and the winter's snow.
In the naked and outcast—seek love there.

—*Anonymous*

## November 20

God is good, God is *good,*
God is so *good,* He's so good to me.
He cares for me, He cares for me,
He cares for me, He's so good to me.

—*Traditional*

## November 21

No longer forward nor behind
I look in hope or fear;
But, grateful, take the good I find,
The best of now and here.

—*John Greenleaf Whittier*

**November 22**

*St. Cecilia's Day,*
*celebrating the patron*
*saint of music*

> I pray and I sing. And sometimes my prayer is my
> singing.
>
> —*Bobby McFerrin*

**November 23**

> Mighty God, Father of all,
> Compassionate God, Mother of all,
> bless every person I have met,
> every face I have seen,
> every voice I have heard,
> especially those most dear;
> bless every city, town, and
> street that I have known,
> bless every sight I have seen,
> every sound I have heard,
> every object I have touched.
> In some mysterious way these
> have all fashioned my life;
> all that I am,
> I have received.
> Great God, bless the world.
>
> —*John J. Morris, SJ*

## November 24

Write the wrongs that are done to you in sand, but write the good things that happen to you on a piece of marble. Let go of all emotions such as resentment and retaliation, which diminish you, and hold onto the emotions, such as gratitude and joy, which increase you.

—*Arabic proverb*

249

## November 25

May God, the Giver of all wisdom, beauty,
    and well-being,
bless all who love Her with these gifts,
and grant that Her blessings may be
    generously shared.

—*Marchiene Vroon Rienstra*

**November 26**

*In 1789, Thanksgiving
is celebrated nationally in
the United States for the
first time*

Gratefulness brings joy to my life. How could I find joy in what I take for granted? So I stop "taking for granted," and there is no end to the surprises I find. A grateful attitude is a creative one, because, in the final analysis, opportunity is the gift within the gift of every moment—the opportunity to see and hear and smell and touch and taste with pleasure.

There is no closer bond than the one that gratefulness celebrates, the bond between giver and thanksgiver. Everything is a gift. Grateful living is a celebration of the universal give-and-take of life, a limitless yes to belonging.

Can our world survive without gratefulness? Whatever the answer, one thing is certain: to say an unconditional yes to the mutual belonging of all beings will make this a more joyful world. This is the reason why yes is my favorite synonym for God.

—*Brother David Steindl-Rast*

## November 27

Be at peace with your own soul, then heaven and
earth will be at peace with you. Enter eagerly into
the treasure house that is within you, you will see
the things that are in heaven; for there is but one
single entry to them both. The ladder that leads to
the Kingdom is hidden within your soul . . . Dive
into yourself, and in your soul you will discover the
stairs by which to ascend.

—*Saint Isaac of Nineveh*

## November 28

May all beings have happiness, and the causes of
    happiness;
May all be free from sorrow, and the causes of
    sorrow;
May all never be separated from the sacred happiness
    which is sorrowless;
And may all live in equanimity, without too much
    attachment and too much aversion,
And live believing in the equality of all that lives.

—*Buddhist prayer*

**November 29**

*U.S. author Madeleine*
*L'Engle is born in 1918*

It is no coincidence that the root word of whole, health, heal, holy, is *hale* (as in *hale and hearty*). If we are healed, we become whole; we are hale and hearty; we are holy.

The marvellous thing is that this holiness is nothing we can earn. We don't become holy by acquiring merit badges and Brownie points. It has nothing to do with virtue or job descriptions or morality. It is nothing we can *do,* in this do-it-yourself world. It is gift, sheer gift, waiting there to be recognized and received. We do not have to be qualified to be holy. We do not have to be qualified to be whole, or healed.

*—Madeleine L'Engle*

**November 30**

You shall ask
What good are dead leaves
And I will tell you
They nourish the sore earth.
You shall ask
What reason is there for winter
And I will tell you
To bring about new leaves.

You shall ask
Why are the leaves so green
And I will tell you
Because they are rich with life.
You shall ask
Why must summer end
And I will tell you
So that the leaves can die.

—*Nancy Wood*

## December 1

Precious Lord, take my hand.
Lead me on. Let me stand.
I am tired. I am weak. I am worn.
Through the storm,
Through the night,
Lead me on to the light.
Take my hand, precious Lord,
and lead me home

—*African-American spiritual*

## December 2

> To go in the dark with a light is to know the light.
> To know the dark, go dark. Go without sight,
> and find that the dark, too, blooms and sings,
> and is traveled by dark feet and dark wings.

> *—Wendell Berry*

## December 3

> The only true wisdom lives far from mankind, out
> in the great loneliness, and it can be reached only
> through suffering. Privation and suffering alone
> can open the mind of a man to all that is hidden
> to others.

> *—Igjugarjuk, 20th-century*
> *Caribou Eskimo shaman*

## December 4

*German poet*
*Rainer Maria*
*Rilke is born*
*in 1875*

> Silent friend of many distances, feel
> how your breath enlarges all of space.

Let your presence ring out like a bell
into the night. What feeds upon your face

grows mighty from the nourishment thus
offered. Move through transformation, out and
in. What is the deepest loss that you have
suffered? If drinking is bitter, change yourself to
wine.

In this immeasurable darkness, be the power
that rounds your senses in their magic ring,
the sense of their mysterious encounter.

And if the earthly no longer knows your name,
whisper to the silent earth: I'm flowing.
To the flashing water say: I am.

> —*Rainer Maria Rilke,*
> *The Sonnets to Orpheus*
> *Translated by JB Leishman*

**December 5**

From the unreal lead me to
the real,
    From darkness lead me to
light
    From death lead me to
immortality.

> —*The Upanishads*

### December 6
*Lebanese poet*
*Kahlil Gibran*
*is born in 1883*

You shall be free indeed
when your days are not
without a care nor your nights
without a want and a grief,
but rather when these things
girdle your life and
yet you rise above them
naked and unbound.

—*Kahlil Gibran*

### December 7

This snowy morning
That black crow
I hate so much...
But he's beautiful!

—*Basho*

### December 8

Speak your truth.
Listen when others speak theirs, too.
When you let go of fear, you will learn to love others,
and you will let them love you.
Do not be afraid of dying.
But do not be afraid to live.
Ask yourself what that means.
Open your heart to love, for that is why you're here.
And know that you are, and always have been One
with Me and all who live.

—*Melody Beattie*

### December 9

Gentle me,
Holy One,
into an unclenched moment,
    a deep breath,
        a letting go
            of heavy experiences,
                of shriveling anxieties,
                    of dead certainties,
that, softened by the silence,
    surrounded by the light,
        and open to the mystery,

I may be found by wholeness
    upheld by the unfathomable,
        entranced by the simple,
            and filled with the joy
                that is you.

—*Ted Loder*

### December 10

Knowing others is intelligence;
knowing yourself is true wisdom.
Mastering others is strength;
mastering yourself is true power.

If you realize that you have enough,
you are truly rich.
If you stay in the center
and embrace death with your whole heart,
you will endure forever.

—*Lao-Tzu*
*Translated by Stephen Mitchell*

**December 11**

*In 1946, the*
*United Nations*
*International Children's*
*Emergency Fund*
*(UNICEF) is founded*

O God of the children of Somalia, Sarajevo, South
     Africa, and South Carolina
Of Albania, Alabama, Bosnia, and Boston,
Of Cracow and Cairo, Chicago and Croatia,
*Help us to love and respect and protect them all.*

O God of Black and Brown and White and Albino
     children and those all mixed together,
Of children who are rich and poor and in between,
Of children who speak English and Spanish and
     Russian and Hmong and languages our ears
     cannot discern,
*Help us to love and respect and protect them all.*

O God of the child prodigy and the child prostitute,
     of the child of rapture and the child of rape,
Of runaway or thrown-away children who struggle
     every day without parent or place or friend
     or future,
*Help us to love and respect and protect them all.*

O God of children who can walk and talk and hear
     and see and sing and dance and jump and

play and of children who wish they could
but can't,
Of children who are loved and unloved, wanted and
unwanted,
*Help us to love and respect and protect them all.*

O God of beggar, beaten, abused, neglected,
homeless, AIDS, drug, and hunger-ravaged
children,
Of children who are emotionally and physically and
mentally fragile,
and of children who rebel and ridicule, torment and
taunt,
*Help us to love and respect and protect them all.*

O God of children of destiny and of despair, of war
and of peace,
Of disfigured, diseased, and dying children,
Of children without hope and of children with hope
to spare and to share,
*Help us to love and respect and protect them all.*

—*Marian Wright Edelman*

### December 12

Dear God,

Help me never to forget this moment. Silence, as
Ross and I trudge our way toward Wellesley Hospital,

heading into bitter wind. People—Asian, Black, Indian, White, old and young—plod through Christmas snowflakes. Lovers drink coffee in restaurant windows. Do they know how beautiful they are? Do they know how poinsettias blaze through the heart in the sheer joy of red? Do they see greenness dancing off live Christmas trees? Do they hear bells? Do they taste snow? Do they smell candles and cider?

Dear God, for the sheer delight of incarnation, much thanks. And for this new child—this new consciousness—born in me this winter night, I thank you.

*—Marion Woodman*
*December 12, 1994*

## December 13

Dear Heavenly One,
Help me accept Love as it is given
even though it may not come
in the package
I requested.

*—Judy Ford*

## December 14

Be still and know that I am God.

*—Psalm 46:10*

## December 15

Busy, normal people: the world is here.
Can you hear it wailing, crying, whispering?
Listen: the world is here.
Don't you hear it,
Praying and sighing and groaning for wholeness?
Sighing and whispering: wholeness,
wholeness, wholeness?
An arduous, tiresome, difficult journey
towards wholeness.
God, who gives us strength of
body, make us whole.
Wholeness of persons: well-being of individuals.
The cry for bodily health and spiritual
strength is echoed from person to
person, from patient to doctor.
It goes out from a soul to its pastor.
We, busy, "normal" people: we are sick.
We yearn to experience wholeness in
our innermost being:
In health and prosperity, we continue
to feel un-well,
Un-fulfilled, or half-filled.
There is a hollowness in our pretended
well-being:
Our spirits cry out for the well-being of
the whole human family.

We pride ourselves in our traditional
communal ideology, our extended family.
The beggars and the mad people in our streets:
—Where are their relatives?
Who is their father? Where is their mother?
We cry for the wholeness of humanity.
But the litany of brokenness is without end.
Black and white;
Rich and poor;
Hausa and Yomba;
Presbyterian and Roman Catholic:
We are all parts of each other,
We yearn to be folded into the fullness
of life—together.
Life, together with the outcast,
The prisoner, the mad woman,
the abandoned child;
Our wholeness is intertwined with their hurt.
Wholeness means healing the hurt,
Working with Christ to heal the hurt,
Seeing and feeling the suffering of others,
Standing alongside them.
Their loss of dignity is not their loss:
It is the loss of our human dignity,
We busy, "normal" people.
The person next to you: with a different
language and culture,
With a different skin or hair color—

It is God's diversity, making an unbroken
rainbow circle—
Our covenant of peace with God, encircling
the whole of humanity.
Christians have to re-enact the miracle
of Good Friday:
The torn veil, the broken walls, the
bridge over the chasm,
The broken wall of hostility between
the Jew and the Gentile.
The wall between sacred and secular?
There is no wall
There is only God at work in the whole;
Heal the sores on the feet;
Salvage the disintegrated personality;
Bind the person back into the whole.
For without that one, we do not have a whole.
Even if there are ninety-nine:
Without that one, we do not have a whole.
God, who gives us strength of
body, make us whole.

*—An African Call for Life*

## December 16

There is no form without the gift of the Mother and the Father. From Father Sky comes your consciousness and Mother Earth is your very bones. To sense the balance of the Mother/Father, Father/Mother within one's own being, one's own nature, is a way to renew the Earth, to renew our hearts, to renew the vision.

—*Dhyani Ywahoo*

## December 17

You can only go halfway
into the darkest forest; then you are coming out
the other side.

—*Chinese proverb*

## December 18

Holy Ones of all ages, comfort those who are without comfort this night, give ease to troubled hearts, restore hope to those that are hopeless and give them the lasting blessing of peace.

As Winter deepens and daylight lessens, I call upon the Spinner of the Seasons to bring the illumination of Samhain's gift to all souls, especially to [names].

May the icy winds and the bright snows of Winter bring space and clarity to all who are heavy-burdened.

I give thanks for the wise qualities of the evergreen trees that have stood by me this day: may you show me how my own heart can be evergreen and growing through winters of doubt and darkness.

—*Caitlin Matthews*

**December 19**

Grace strikes us when we are in great pain and restlessness. It strikes us when we walk through the dark valley of a meaningless and empty life. It strikes us when our disgust for our own being, our indifference, our weakness, our hostility, and our lack of direction and composure have become intolerable to us. It strikes us when, year after year, the longed-for perfection of life does not appear, when the old compulsions reign within us as they have for decades, when despair destroys all joy and courage. Sometimes at that moment a wave of light breaks into our darkness, and it is as though a voice were saying: "You are accepted."

—*Paul Tillich*

## December 20

We attend in silence and in joy.
This is the day when healing comes to us.
This is the day when separation ends,
and we remember Who we really are.

—*From A Course in Miracles*
*(Text, page 172)*

# ACKNOWLEDGMENTS

THE FIRST ROUND OF THANKS GOES TO Mary Jane Ryan, for nurturing my seed idea and planting it in the garden of Conari Press, as well as for reminding me of the importance of honoring natural rhythms as *Prayers for Healing* took root. Special thanks to Claudia Schaab for her numerous acts of support, grace and kindness throughout the production of this book.

Many thanks go to my wonderful colleagues at the Institute of Noetic Sciences, particularly Carole Angermeier for her wise counsel; Marilyn Schlitz for her enthusiastic support; Keith Thompson for his insightful suggestions; Jonathan Mathis for his generously shared computer expertise; Barbara McNeill for her keen eyes; and Nola Lewis and Christian de Quincey for their soulful contributions.

Thanks also to those friends old and new who supported me in sundry and special ways during the production of the book: Inez d'Arcy Francis, Kathy Kidd, Joni Goldman, Pardis Amirshahi, Haleh Pourafzal, Jean Deeds, Sharon Lehrer, Judith Cornell, Susannah Arnold and Laurie Bish. Additional thanks to Carl Oman for his technical (and brotherly) support.

Special thanks go to the writers who supported this project by taking the time out of their busy schedules to contribute original prayers: Marion Woodman, Gerald Jampolsky, Rachel Naomi Remen, Hugh Prather, Daphne Rose Kingma, Belleruth Naparstek, Diane Cirincione, Judy Ford, Alan Cohen, Jack Kornfield, and Jacquelyn Small. Thanks also to Deepak Chopra, Angeles Arrien, Carolyn Myss, and Frances Vaughan for suggesting prayers, as well as to the number of Institute of Noetic Sciences members who shared their hearts, ideas and words with me. Finally, my deepest appreciation goes to Dr. Larry Dossey for the beneficence of his foreword and to His Holiness the Dalai Lama for the blessing of his introduction.

# INDEX

278

and HarperCollins Publishers, Inc. All performance, derivative, adaptation, musical, audio and recording, illustrative, theatrical, film, pictorial, electronic and all other rights reserved.

Prayer from *Alcoholics Anonymous*, page 63, is reprinted with the permission of Alcoholics Anonymous World Services Inc. Permission to reprint this material does not mean that A.A. is in any way affiliated with this program. A.A. is a program of recovery from alcoholism only–use of this material in connections with programs and activities which are patterned after A.A., but which address other problems, or in any other non–A.A. context, does not imply otherwise.

Excerpt from *Wrestling the Light: Ache and Awe in the Human-Divine Struggle* by Ted Loder, copyright © 1991 Innisfree Press, reprinted by permission of Innisfree Press, Philadelphia, Pennsylvania, U.S.A.

Excerpt from *Guerrillas of Grace: Prayers for the Battle* by Ted Loder, copyright © 1984 Innisfree Press, reprinted by permission of Innisfree Press, Philadelphia, Pennsylvania, U.S.A.

Selections by Martin Luther King, Jr., reprinted by arrangement with The Heirs to the Estate of Martin Luther King, Jr., c/o Writers House, Inc. as agent for the proprietor. Copyright © 1963 by Martin Luther King, Jr., copyright renewed 1991 by Coretta Scott King.

293

## ABOUT THE INSTITUTE OF NOETIC SCIENCES

A portion of proceeds from this book will go to the Institute of Noetic Sciences.

The Institute of Noetic Sciences, founded in 1973, is a research foundation, an educational institution, and a membership organization. The word "noetic" is derived from the Greek word *nous,* meaning mind, intelligence, or ways of knowing. Noetic sciences study the mind and its diverse ways of knowing in a truly interdisciplinary fashion.

As a research foundation, we provide small grants for leading-edge scientific and scholarly research. Our intention is that results from these pilot studies will encourage other funding sources to generate larger research projects. In this way, important new ideas gain legitimacy.

As an educational institution, we organize lectures, sponsor conferences, and publish books, research reports and monographs by leading scientists, philosophers, and scholars. We also publish the *Noetic Sciences Review* and other publications, resources and tools for transformation. We support and stimulate individuals and organizations interested in discovering and legitimizing new belief systems which embrace human potential for healing, creativity, and wholeness.

As a membership organization, we offer opportunities for individuals to blend knowledge of scientific and scholarly research with their own experiences. Members receive regular Institute publications and are invited to participate in community groups, lectures, and field research. Our travel program offers exploration of diverse cultures around the world. Through these activities, we are creating and bringing legitimacy to a vision of a humane, sustainable, and peaceful world.

To find out more about the Institute of
Noetic Sciences and its programs,
please call
1 800 · 383 · 1394

We are looking for personal stories to include in a book on prayers that have been answered.

If you have, or know of, such an account, please send your story or suggestion to:

Maggie Oman
"Answered Prayers"
c/o Red Wheel/Weiser/Conari Press
500 Third Street, Suite 230
San Francisco, CA 94107

Sending of a piece grants Maggie Oman the right to edit and publish it.

Conari Press, established in 1987, publishes books on topics
ranging from spirituality and women's history to sexuality and
personal growth. Our main goal is to publish quality books
that will make a difference in people's lives—both
how we feel about ourselves and how
we relate to one another.

Our readers are our most important resource, and we
value your input, suggestions, and ideas. We'd love to
hear from you—after all, we are
publishing books for you!

For a complete catalog or to be added to
our mailing list, please contact us at:

CONARI PRESS
500 Third Street, Suite 230
San Francisco, CA 94107
*www.conari.com*